THE *Greatest* GIFT

A Collection
Devoted to Prayer

ॐ

BRUCE WILKINSON	*OLIVER NORTH*
RUTH MYERS	*SHIRLEY DOBSON*
OTIS LEDBETTER	*RON MEHL*
DAVID JEREMIAH	*GREG LAURIE*

THE GREATEST GIFT

published by Multnomah Publishers, Inc.

© 2006 by Multnomah Publishers, Inc.

International Standard Book Number: 1-59052-737-2

Scripture quotations are from:

The Holy Bible, New International Version (NIV) © 1973, 1984 by International Bible Society, used by permission of Zondervan Publishing House

New American Standard Bible (NASB) 1960, 1977, 1995 by the Lockman Foundation. Used by permission.

The Holy Bible, New King James Version (NKJV) © 1984 by Thomas Nelson, Inc.

Holy Bible, New Living Translation (NLT) © 1996. Used by permission of Tyndale House Publishers, Inc. All rights reserved.

New American Standard Bible® (NASB) © 1960, 1977, 1995 by the Lockman Foundation. Used by permission.

The Living Bible (TLB) © 1971. Used by permission of Tyndale House Publishers, Inc. All rights reserved.

The Amplified Bible (AMP) © 1965, 1987 by Zondervan Publishing House.

Multnomah is a trademark of Multnomah Publishers, Inc., and is registered in the U.S. Patent and Trademark Office.

The colophon is a trademark of Multnomah Publishers, Inc.

Printed in the United States of America

For information:

MULTNOMAH PUBLISHERS, INC.
601 N. LARCH ST.
SISTERS, OREGON 97759

06 07 08 09 10—10 9 8 7 6 5 4 3 2 1

OUR GREATEST GIFT

DAVID JEREMIAH

What's the most wonderful gift in God's great big bag of blessings for us here on earth?

For me, I've found that greatest blessing to be prayer. I believe each of us has a tremendous potential for God through the ministry of praying. It's something attainable by all of us as believers, no matter who we are or what our life circumstances. I'm speaking of something wonderful and joyous and indescribable. It's something God designed to bless us beyond all imagining. And yet it is easily within our reach as a thrilling, daily adventure.

But I must confess to you that prayer can be the hardest work I do, and I suspect there are times when you feel the same way. Even the disciples who lived and walked with Jesus must have had many of the same frustrations with prayer you and I have. Why else would they have come to their Master one day and asked, "Lord, please show us how to pray"?

Why the Struggle?

Why is prayer so often difficult? And why does consistent prayer take such discipline on our part?

When I began a battle against cancer a few years ago, I learned something about prayer, and I know of no better way to say it than this: There's prayer, and then there's *prayer*. When things are going smoothly in your life, you pray one way; when you get into a tight spot, you pray another way. Your pleas become more intense; you find yourself crying out to God.

I believe God wants us to pray earnestly like that all the time, on both good days and bad. However, that kind of prayer just doesn't come naturally to us on a regular basis. That's where the discipline comes in. I'm convinced that until we get serious about prayer, we won't know the half of our Lord's desire for our lives.

_____

From *The Prayer Matrix,* Introduction

COME

"Come to me, all who labor and are heavy laden,
and I will give you rest."

MATTHEW 11:28

Seek the LORD while he may be found;
call upon him while he is near.

ISAIAH 55:6

Let us then with confidence draw near
to the throne of grace,
that we may receive mercy
and find grace to help in time of need.

HEBREWS 4:16

CHAPTER I

OUT OF THE CHAOS, INTO THE CALM

J. OTIS LEDBETTER

෨෬

For those who trust in You...
You shall hide them
in the secret place of Your presence.

PSALM 31:19—20

Especially when danger swirled around him, David—the man after God's own heart—learned to cherish his own secret place in the Lord's presence. Look at how he sings about it in the twenty-seventh Psalm:

For in the time of trouble
He shall hide me in His pavilion;
In the secret place of His tabernacle
He shall hide me. (v. 5)

In the secret place, David becomes totally aware of being completely protected—and that same experience can also be yours.

In the secret place you can find full assurance of personal victory in the Lord, just as David does: "He shall set me high upon a rock. And now my head shall be lifted up above my enemies all around me" (vv. 5–6).

Are you facing any threat or hardship at this time that makes you anxious or fearful? In the secret place you can recover the same fresh awareness of God and the same ability to cast off fear that David sings about in this psalm. Just listen to his God-given confidence:

> The LORD is my light and my salvation;
> Whom shall I fear?
> The LORD is the strength of my life;
> Of whom shall I be afraid?...
> Though an army may encamp against me,
> My heart shall not fear;
> Though war should rise against me,
> In this I will be confident. (vv. 1, 3)

THE ONE THING WE DESIRE

For David—and for you and me—the secret place is more than a place of protection and confidence building. It's the environment for resting in the very dwelling place of God, the very presence of God.

David describes his secret place as an entry into God's "pavilion" and "tabernacle" (Psalm 27:5); it ushers him into "the house of the Lord" and "His temple" (v. 4). In David's lifetime, the glorious and beautiful temple that would rise on Mount Zion in Jerusalem had not yet been constructed; David's eyes at this moment are on a place even more glorious and beautiful, the temple in heaven where he communes with God by way of the secret place. Your eyes can look there too.

Your own secret place is where you, like David, can "behold the beauty of the LORD" (v. 4)—enjoying your unique individual experience of God as He reveals Himself to you with an intimacy that brings more inner satisfaction than anything else possibly could. In such intimacy you can "inquire in His temple," just as David does (v. 4), laying before Him your every need, your every concern, your every question, and finding God's help and answers.

No wonder David joyfully concludes that being with God in the secret place is the "one thing" he desires of the Lord, the ultimate experience he seeks (v. 4). This will be your lasting desire as well, as you continue to meet with God in the secret place.

Prescription for Peace

In the Bible, my favorite look inside the secret place comes in Psalm 91, a passage I strongly urge you to turn to as soon as possible as you explore and get acquainted with your secret place. Allow God to personalize the message of this psalm for you, engraving it into your soul as a vision and a guarantee of the blessedness He has in store for you there.

The unnamed author of this psalm gives us a guided tour of a restful, safe place that's like a veritable oasis for the longing or fearful spirit. In this place, chaos is absent, calmness is in abundance. It's a prescription for peace from the Great Physician.

Rest…safety…calmness…peace…. For most of us, those words don't exactly describe life as usual. Why is that?

Have you ever thought about how much of our lives is influenced by potentially negative forces outside our control? Listen to how the worst of such harmful uncertainties are vividly depicted in Psalm 91:

The snare…

The terror by night…

The arrow that flies by day…

The pestilence that walks in darkness…

The destruction that lays waste at noonday. (vv. 3–6)

Chilling terms—yet fully on the mark in describing how we can sometimes feel about the unexpected battles and challenges that flare up against us in life and corner our attention.

TRAPPED BY THE UNCONTROLLABLE

When you think about it, isn't our anxiety over such uncontrollable factors and circumstances the very thing that often keeps us from accomplishing great things for God? Doesn't it hinder us from realizing our potential in Christ and pull us back from giving our best effort in whatever He calls us to?

We get trapped: "Like birds caught in a snare, so the sons of men are snared in an evil time, when it falls suddenly upon them" (Ecclesiastes 9:12).

Psalm 91 goes on to give another frightful image you may identify with: "A thousand may fall at your side, and ten thousand at your right hand" (v. 7). Have you noticed how the failures of others around you—spiritual failures, moral failures, relational failures, career failures, ministry failures—can dampen and wither your own motivation for success and accomplishment and your sense of security about the future? So many lives around us are littered with disappointments and breakdowns, causing us to shy away ourselves from indulging in big dreams, from reaching for the stars and risking any part of life to accomplish big things. Our personal goals that once shone so brightly now seem too lofty and unrealistic.

THE SHADOW THAT PROTECTS

So many discouraging obstacles in life, so many potential adversities! But you're responding properly to them when you let those fears and concerns drive you to the secret place, to reinforce its deepest lesson:

> *He who dwells in the secret place of the Most High*
> *Shall abide under the shadow of the Almighty. (91:1)*

The secret place is where you deepen your capacity to abide calmly in Christ, to live constantly within His shadow.

By dwelling in the secret place, your faith in God will be energized. From the depths of your being, you'll sing along with the author of this psalm, "He is my refuge and my fortress; my God, in Him I will trust" (v. 2).

And what about those uncontrollable adversities, all that danger by day and danger by night? "Surely He shall deliver you…. You shall not be afraid" (vv. 3, 5).

Resting in the secret place, you'll find the bold conviction and confidence to hold on to the following words as your personal promise from God:

> *No evil shall befall you,*
> *Nor shall any plague come near your dwelling. (v. 10)*

And what about all the failure that strikes down so many others all around you? "It shall not come near you" (v. 7)!

With the eyes of your heart, this is how you'll see yourself in the enfolding protection of your loving God:

He shall cover you with His feathers,
And under His wings you shall take refuge;
His truth shall be your shield and buckler. (v. 4)

Through the time you spend in the secret place, you'll also come to believe firmly in the reality and presence of God's guardian angels and their power in your own life and experience:

For He shall give His angels charge over you,
To keep you in all your ways.
In their hands they shall bear you up,
Lest you dash your foot against a stone. (91:11–12)

GLIMPSING YOUR FUTURE

What's more, in the secret place your God-nurtured plans and His calling for your future will spring to life in your spiritual vision, and you'll be assured of vanquishing spiritual foes as you move forward in God's kingdom work and in spiritual warfare:

You shall tread upon the lion and the cobra,
The young lion and the serpent you shall trample
*   underfoot. (v. 13)*

Abiding in the secret place, you'll hear the words of Jesus as never before: "Behold, I give you the authority to trample on serpents and scorpions, and over all the power of the enemy, and nothing shall by any means hurt you" (Luke 10:19). The secret place is where your innermost spirit will get reconnected to the truth that if God is for you, no one can be against you (Romans 8:31).

These are the soaring promises and solid provisions for the man or woman who will abide with God in the secret place.

So go to the secret place, and let your loving Father personally deliver those promises to your heart!

———————

From *In the Secret Place*, Chapter 3

CHAPTER 2

AN INVITATION TO PRAY

RUTH MYERS

ॐ

The telephone rings and it's your country's leader. He wants to come by for a visit. While you try not to gasp into the phone, he continues. He hopes to find out if there's some way he can help you. And he wants to talk personally with you about a project on a scale almost beyond imagining—an undertaking he'd like you to be a part of.

How would you feel after such a call?

"Well," you say, "I'd feel shocked, a bit intimidated—and a bit doubtful about his motives."

Yes, but wouldn't you also feel honored? Wouldn't your life suddenly seem more significant? All your daily strivings a little less humdrum? As you waited nervously for your president or prime minister to visit, wouldn't you see yourself in a completely different light?

The King of all kings, the Ruler of the entire universe, has already made that call. He wants time with you. He wants you to tell Him about your needs and interests. And He's asking for your partnership on an immensely important project.

If you've picked up this book, we're sure you're like so many Christians we've met. You sincerely long for that "closer, more fruitful walk with God." You also feel a deep concern for our hurting, disintegrating, fragmented world and the people in it—starting with your family, your friends, and your coworkers. And you want to be part of what God wants to do in people's lives and in our world.

What God has in mind begins with prayer. And His invitation to pray lies at the very heart of His loving best for each of us.

Why God Planned Prayer

Have you ever wondered why God chose to link His actions with our praying? Why did he decide that our prayers would cause Him to accomplish certain things or expand what He does? And that by not praying we would limit Him? Could He not have carried out His purpose far more efficiently without us? Yet He has established the prayers of His people as a powerful influence on how and when He meets our needs (material, emotional, spiritual) and the needs of others throughout the world.

The answer goes back to why God created us. He created us to be His loved ones, His family with whom He can share a relationship of mutual enjoyment. This shows the kind of God He is—a personal God who values loving relationships more than anything else in all the universe. Before He ever created angels and people, He was a "three-person" God—Father, Son, and Holy Spirit—living in perfect love and unbroken fellowship. He created us to be part of His inner circle of love, for both His delight and ours.

God longs to express His boundless love by meeting our needs to the point of overflowing. Even if we don't pray, He still holds together every molecule in our bodies; He is still the source of every good thing. But prayer keeps us aware of Him as our Source and opens our lives to receive His greater bounty. Prayer also links our lives with God's exciting purposes and power. More importantly, it brings us into a love relationship with God, rooted in our realizing how much we need Him and our choosing to depend on Him. The more we pray, the more we're able to let God meet our emotional and spiritual needs and love others through us. Prayer ushers us into an experience with God, a growing sense of wonder, delight, and gratefulness.

THE REWARDS OF "GIVING" PRAYERS

Praying for others is a form of giving, and praying for God's best in our lives is part of giving ourselves to Him. As we form the habit of "giving" prayers, we start growing out of our natural tendency to major on "give me" prayers. We accept God's call to be partners with Him, with the high privilege of drawing people into His inner circle of love. We step into a larger arena of prayer, where we learn to pray more broadly, with God's purposes firmly in mind. We respond to the King's invitation when He said, "I'm up to something far more momentous than you might have supposed in your life, in the lives of your loved ones, and in the whole world—and I'm asking you to be part of it."

This lifts us out of the puny reasons for living that we humans invent apart from Him.

You may be wondering if there's something unacceptable about praying for everyday personal and family concerns—health, money, protection. Absolutely not. Jesus Himself taught us to pray, "Give us this day our daily bread." We follow His example when we acknowledge our need for God's down-to-earth favors and help.

God loves to hear you talk with Him about yourself and the people you love. He wants you to pray about your personal needs.

Yet this is not all there is to prayer. A child asking his dad for candy or a hamburger is not all there is to a growing relationship of love between him and his father. The Lord's Prayer has seven requests; six of them relate to God's purposes and to our spiritual needs, one to our practical needs. And the apostle

Paul's prayers center largely on helping believers experience God and spiritual realities.

All kinds of prayers delight God—worship and thanksgiving, confessing our sins, quiet communion, praying for our own multilevel needs (often called petition), and praying for our loved ones and other people (intercession). All are part of mature praying—part of our wonderful privilege of conversing with the awesome, all-powerful Person who is our Father and our Friend.

THE PRIVILEGE OF ROYAL PRAYING

There is also the privilege of intercessory prayer—what we like to call "royal praying." It is praying along with the King of kings in His loving plans to bring relief and blessing and spiritual power to countless people. When we intercede we become prayer partners with Christ, who is always interceding before the Father (Hebrews 7:25). We join Him in His inner circle of prayer, where our prayers embrace His deepest longings as well as our own. And we get answers that make a tremendous difference now and forever.

Though we don't pray for others just to get blessed, intercessory prayer does bring extraordinary blessings our way. As always with God, we receive more than we give, and we become more than we are. We become part of the most significant undertaking of all time—the work of redemption that God has been doing for centuries. Breaking through the comfortable ways that fence us in, we gain a new sense of significance and fulfillment. And besides all this, we lay up tremendous rewards for eternity.

Jesus promised, "Give and it shall be given unto you." *Giving* prayer is one way of spending ourselves for others. It puts us in place to receive more of what God promises in many Scriptures, such as Isaiah 58:10–11: "If you spend yourselves in behalf of the hungry and satisfy the needs of the oppressed, then your light will rise in the darkness, and your night will become like the noonday. The LORD will guide you always: he will satisfy your needs in a sun-scorched land and will strengthen your frame. You will be like a well-watered garden, like a spring whose waters never fail."

You Can Make a Difference

Intercession makes impossible things possible, not only in our own households but also in faraway places.

For years in upper New York, a bedridden young woman prayed earnestly for a nomadic pygmy tribe in Africa. Ten years after she died, the tribe was reached by Gospel Recordings, Inc. with an incredible turning to Christ. For decades William Carey, considered the father of modern mission, sent detailed prayer requests from India to his invalid sister in England. She prayed over them with great diligence, and God used Carey in history-making ways.

In God's eyes, who gets the rewards for the amazing conversion of that pygmy tribe? And for Carey's remarkable work in India? We find a clue in 1 Samuel 30:24, where King David decreed: "The share of the man who stayed with the supplies is to be the same as that of him who went down to the battle. All will share alike."

Early this century S. D. Gordon, the well-known devotional writer, wrote:

> *The great people of the earth today are the people*
> *who pray. I do not mean those who talk about prayer,*
> *nor those who say they believe in prayer, nor yet those*
> *who can explain about prayer, but I mean those*
> *people who take time and pray. They have not time.*
> *It must be taken from something else. This something*
> *else is important. Very important, and pressing, but*
> *still less important and less pressing than prayer.*

GOD'S INVITATION TO PRAY

When you thought of getting that phone call from your nation's top leader, perhaps you felt a bit fearful, a bit threatened. Maybe you feel the same way when you contemplate God's invitation to pray and intercede. The idea of adding yet another requirement to your hectic schedule sounds like just another setup for failure.

"I'd love to pray more. But how?" you ask. "The last thing I need is more guilt!"

Perhaps you're in a season of life when more time for prayer seems like the impossible dream. Maybe you're a student with a heavy load, a mother with small children, a breadwinner working long hours, the caregiver for someone with a long-term illness or disability. Yet a richer prayer life can still be yours.

The good news is that we're not talking about spending hours in prayer. We're inviting you to invest ten to fifteen minutes a day to grow in prayer. And we'll show you how. Our aim is to encourage and help you, not to pressure you with guilt.

Sometimes God calls one of His children into an intensive, major ministry of prayer. Wonderful! Yet there's a blessed middle ground between intercession as a life work and no praying at all. In fact, we find there are many middle grounds in prayer that please the Lord. Like a loving earthly father, God always welcomes us into His presence, and He honors us when we show that we care and we try. Remember, prayer starts with a personal relationship, not with performance. Our fearful expectations probably come from our own confusion or from Satan, our day-and-night accuser (Revelation 12:10).

God's call to pray is an invitation to success. When we pray, we're succeeding in God's eyes. He then takes charge of the results of our praying, and He cannot fail. In His Word He has promised to hear and answer prayer. Our prayers may sometimes seem insignificant in our eyes, but they are not insignificant in God's eyes.

The time you can set aside for prayer may seem small. But it will help you develop an attitude of prayer. Then you'll be able more and more to supplement your set-apart times of prayer with on-the-go prayers throughout the day. Many important answers to prayer come through such praying—and it can flourish in the busiest of schedules. Beginning to nurture some praying in your life, as it is right now, can become the launching pad for more later.

HELP ALONG THE WAY

God doesn't give a command, "Pray!" and then, like a drill sergeant, stand back to see if we'll obey, or come by only to inspect how well we're doing. He invites us—welcomes us—into the high privilege of talking and laboring with Him. He provides us with the enabling power of the Holy Spirit within us and gives us guidance for fruitful prayer in the Bible. He then encourages us through other Christians who may be a bit farther along the road than we are.

Consider this book part of the Lord's encouragement to you. It will guide you in your new prayer adventure.

From *31 Days of Prayer*, Part 1

Chapter 3

Declaration of Dependence

David Jeremiah

Years ago, at a time when I needed a break from a hectic schedule, my family took a quick trip up to Lake Arrowhead in the San Bernardino Mountains of Southern California. It was a wonderful, refreshing recovery time. Somehow when you go to the mountains, it helps clear your head, and as I hiked around that weekend, I did a lot of thinking.

I understood, maybe for the first time, why it's so critical to develop a strong and deep relationship with Jesus Christ. I realized there's simply no other relationship on earth that can meet our ultimate needs. That's no fault of ours or anyone else's. It's simply how we were created. We may think it's unfair, but it's just the way life is. It's a part of that matrix we're discovering.

As I walked around Lake Arrowhead on that occasion, I wrote something down. Here it is: "Jesus Christ, the same yesterday, today, and forever." If we put our hopes and pour our lives into anything else besides Him, it's certain that we'll be ultimately disappointed. But if we put our hopes and pour our lives into Jesus Christ, we'll ultimately find far more fulfillment and blessing than we can ever imagine.

BIG PROBLEMS, BIG SOLUTIONS

Sometimes we can get so overwhelmed and discouraged by the desperate needs and difficulties we experience in our lives. But could it be that one reason we have great problems is that God wants to show us great solutions? He longs to show us the riches of His grace and the poverty of our own resources. Prayer is uniquely designed to demonstrate both truths.

That's why God encourages us with these words: "Let us therefore come boldly to the throne of grace, that we may obtain mercy and find grace to help in time of need" (Hebrews 4:16).

Prayer and our times of need go hand in hand.

SHUT UP

When I battled cancer, the lesson I learned that struck home with most force was this: *I discovered I was helpless without God.* I learned how to pray out of desperation.

In *Fresh Wind, Fresh Fire,* Jim Cymbala said something I can easily identify with: "Prayer cannot truly be taught by principles and seminars and symposiums. It has to be born out of a whole environment of felt need. If I say, 'I *ought* to pray,' I will soon run out of motivation and quit; the flesh is too strong. I have to be *driven* to pray."

And Andrew Bonar wrote this: "God likes to see His people shut up to this: That there is no hope but in prayer."

At least initially, serious prayer is almost always driven by such desperate necessity. We don't pray because we ought to; we pray because we are without any other recourse. I think God likes to see His people coming to Him in desperation and casting themselves upon His mercy. Only then do we recognize reality for what it is.

KEEP BUZZING THE NURSE

One day I finally recognized with particular clarity why it was so hard for me to pray, and that day I wrote this down in my Bible: "Prayer is my Declaration of Dependence." For a go-getter, type A, driven person like me, prayer is difficult because it flies in the face of our frantic efforts to prove that we're self-sufficient, independent, and strong. With prayer I have to admit I'm spiritually impotent.

John Piper calls prayer "the antidote for the disease of self-confidence." He then goes on to point out a telling difference between Uncle Sam and Jesus Christ: "Uncle Sam won't enlist you in his service unless you are healthy, and Jesus won't enlist you unless you are sick." It's just as Jesus said: "Those who are well have no need of a physician, but those who are sick. I did not come to call the righteous, but sinners, to repentance" (Mark 2:17).

Piper then notes that "Christianity is fundamentally convalescence ('Pray without ceasing' = Keep buzzing the nurse)."

My bout with cancer taught me a lot about "buzzing the nurse"! The fears and desperation which forced me to my knees taught me to cry out to God as never before. And do you know what? God heard! He answered! He delivered me from all my fears. And I know He desires to do the same for you.

IT'S THE TRUTH

We become men and women of prayer when we recognize our desperate need. Our culture teaches that we don't need God because we ourselves are god. Prayer stabs at the heart of that idea. God tells us that we're dependent upon Him, and He doesn't say that just to lord it over us; He's telling the truth, and we can either accept it by faith or have to learn this lesson the hard way through the difficulties of life.

One day I recorded the following in my journal:

I am writing these prayers to You because my mind so easily wanders from the thought process when I

*pray in another way. I want to be working things
out with You in my prayer time, and I believe that
I am learning how to do that, at least in some
measure. I realize more than ever before that this
time is more important than sermon preparation, or
even than the preaching of a sermon. If I do not
work things out with You, I am doomed to failure
and frustration and fatigue!*

I have learned, and am learning, that there's no real victory or joy in the Christian life unless there's also a sense of total dependence upon God. And that sense of dependence is what makes prayer spring to life.

Think about it: When Jesus walked upon this earth as both God and man, He lived as a man in dependence upon His Father, giving us an example of how we're to live. And if Jesus Christ, with all His power and perfection, made prayer a priority in His life, then where ought prayer to fit in your life and in mine?

ESPECIALLY THE BASICS

We depend upon God for everything, of course—for breath, for life, for companionship, for emotional support, for spiritual guidance, for vision, for hope. As Paul said to the philosophers in Athens, God gives to everyone "life, breath, and all things" (Acts 17:25).

And to help us remember all that, Jesus taught us to focus in prayer on our dependence on God for the daily supply of our material needs: "Give us this day our daily bread" (Matthew 6:11).

When Jesus told us to pray that, He especially had in mind the physical necessities of life represented by bread. The only reason we don't all die of starvation is that God is good and provides us with the food we need.

In Matthew 4:4, Jesus responded to one of the devil's temptations in the wilderness by quoting from Deuteronomy 8:3 and saying, "Man shall not live by bread alone, but by every word that proceeds from the mouth of God."

There's more to that verse than the simple truth that spiritual things are more important than material things. Bread itself would have no value to us unless its value had been supplied by the Creator.

Why is it that bread meets the needs of the human body? How is it that the plants which grow from the earth have the ability to supply us with strength? How can they help us to grow? It's possible only through the word that proceeds out of the mouth of God. God speaks, and grain is given its nutritional properties. Were God to withdraw His word, bread would be useless to us; we might as well eat gravel.

It's the very word of God that sustains us. Hebrews 1:3 tells us that Christ is "upholding all things by the word of His power." And Paul told us that in Christ "all things hold together" (Colossians 1:17). There's nothing more basic to meeting our basic needs than the Word of God.

On, In, Over

What are our basic needs? Essentially, we need something to put on us, something to put in us, and something to put over us. God says He'll take care of all three for us if we trust Him. And as part of trusting Him, He wants us to ask Him for these things every day.

God wants us to ask for our daily bread not because He wants to hear us beg, but because He knows we have short memories and often forget that He's the One who supplies our every need. Praying daily for our bread helps fight our pride and materialism.

George Mueller knew all about asking for bread, and he saw God provide time after time in astonishing ways. I treasure the poem he crafted in response to God's faithfulness:

> *I believe God answers prayer,*
> *Answers always, everywhere;*
> *I may cast my anxious care,*
> *Burdens I could never bear,*
> *On the God who heareth prayer.*

Never need my soul despair
Since He bids me boldly dare
To the secret place repair,
There to prove He answers prayer.

POINTEDLY, SPECIFICALLY

I talk with Christian people all the time who are in the midst of severe trials. Sometimes I ask them, "Have you ever asked God pointedly and specifically—naming the details of the situation—to help you and deliver you?" They often admit that they've prayed in general, though not specifically. But if you're in the lion's den, you need to pray about the lion; if you're in the fire, you need to pray about the flames.

Perhaps you're going through some particular struggles in your life right now, something very demanding and unsettling, and you wonder how God is going to take care of you.

But if you aren't facing a trial at present, let me at least ask you this: What is it that you need now in your life more than anything else?

Name it.

Now...allow me to ask a pointed question. Have you asked God for this? Have you *really* asked Him?

And if you're undergoing a time of serious testing, have you asked God to provide exactly what you need to get through it? Have you prayed for Him to deliver you? Ask Him to do what He did for so many in the Bible. God still delivers! He's the same yesterday, today, and forever.

Maybe you need deliverance from fear. Sometimes, suddenly and out of nowhere, a spirit of fear grips my heart and I have to drop everything, leave my office, and go to a place I know by a lake. I talk and tell God about my fear, asking Him to deliver me from it.

Do you have any fears today? Have you asked God to take it away and to give you His peace and the strength that comes from knowing His presence?

You can say, "God, this situation is beyond me. I can't cope with it. But You can. Please extend Your hand, and help me and deliver me." Then tell Him all that you need.

There's no sickness that God cannot heal. There's no problem God cannot solve. There's no challenge God cannot meet. There's no financial deficit that God cannot overcome. There's no man who can overthrow God's purposes. There's no committee that can thwart God's work in the church of Jesus Christ.

So in prayer before His throne, make your declaration of dependence today...and every day.

———————————

From *The Prayer Matrix,* Chapter 6

CHAPTER 4

WALKING IN GRACE AND MERCY

RON MEHL

☙

And Jehoshaphat feared,
and set himself to seek the LORD.

2 CHRONICLES 20:3

You and I are creatures of time. Even the wisest, brightest, and most perceptive among us cannot see beyond the present moment. For all of the technical brilliance of our scientists and inventors, no one has found a way to peer even two seconds into the future. As James wrote, "Why, you do not even know what will happen tomorrow. What is your life? You are a mist that appears for a little while and then vanishes" (James 4:14).

When we open our eyes each morning, we have no idea what the next twenty-four hours will bring. When I was in Bible college, I remember a professor with a reputation for suddenly springing pop quizzes on the class. Those things were murder. You didn't have the option of waiting until two or three days before the big midterm and final exams to cram your head full of facts. You knew that on any given day, you might walk into his class and find yourself staring at a quiz, testing your knowledge of every reading in the textbook and everything he'd covered in class up to that point.

How unfair can you get? You had to study *every night* for this guy's class. You had to take notes every day, read the assignments every day, and review the material every day, or you might find yourself caught short in the moment of testing.

Jehoshaphat found himself staring at the biggest test of his life, and he had no time to cram, review his notes, speed-read the text, or collect his thoughts.

The enemy was on his doorstep.

Jehoshaphat's great-great-grandfather, Solomon, once wrote: "If you faint in the day of adversity, your strength is small" (Proverbs 24:10). But when is that day of adversity? When will it come? Will there be any warning? Any premonition? King Jehoshaphat had no advance notice, and when trouble crashed into his life, he was gripped with fear. It shook him to the core. It must have felt like a punch in the stomach.

He staggered. He groaned. But he didn't faint.

Instead, he turned instantly to the God of his fathers and poured out his heart.

What kept Jehoshaphat from fainting in the day of testing? What kept him from flying into a blind terror or tumbling into a bottomless despair? How was he able to turn to the Lord the way he did and trust God with this fearful news?

Jehoshaphat's secret was simple. When it came time to run for the Lord's help, he didn't have very far to go. In fact, he walked with God every day. When the messenger burst into the king's court with his dire news, Jehoshaphat didn't have to scramble around looking for the Lord's phone number: *Now, where did I leave that thing? Was it in my old address book? Didn't I keep it on a note in the top drawer? Didn't I see it on a sticky note on the fridge?*

The Lord and Jehoshaphat had probably already been in conversation that day—perhaps that very hour. It was completely natural for the king to turn to God in this moment of fear and distress. Imagine yourself walking with Jesus Christ along the road. Suddenly a lion leaps out of the brush and confronts you. What do you do? You instinctively grasp the Lord's arm and cry out, "Jesus, help me!"

You don't have to make an appointment to see a counselor, and you don't have to check out a book on fear management from the library, because Jesus Himself is right beside you, and you've been conversing with Him all morning long. The more you remain in conversation with the Lord throughout the day, the more "available" you will find Him when you run headlong into a trial. The more you study and read and meditate on His Word, the closer those words will be to your heart when you fall into crisis.

How do we know that Jehoshaphat walked with God? The evidence is right there in Scripture. Second Chronicles 17 tells us that "the LORD was with Jehoshaphat, because he walked in the former ways of his great-great-great grandfather David; he did not seek the Baals, but sought the God of his father, and walked in His commandments" (vv. 3–4).

The king had certainly made a terrible error in judgment when he allied himself—both militarily and maritally—with the evil king Ahab of Israel. Yet even when he was in battle at Ahab's side, and the enemies' chariot captains surrounded him, "Jehoshaphat cried out, and the LORD helped him" (2 Chronicles 18:31).

Upon his return to Jerusalem, the king felt the sting of the Lord's rebuke for that foolish decision, and his family would reap terrible consequences in the years to come. Nevertheless, the prophet Jehu told him, "Good things are found in you, in that you have removed the wooden images from the land and have prepared your heart to seek God" (2 Chronicles 19:3).

The New International Version renders that last verse, *"You…have set your heart on seeking God."* Those who set their hearts on seeking God every day don't have to look up His address in the day of trouble. Those who cultivate the presence of God as a daily habit of life don't have to start from scratch when they need Him the most.

The Bible says, "Seek the LORD and His strength; Seek His face *continually.*" (Psalm 105:4). In other words, we're to go looking for the Lord's strength every day and every hour of the day—not just when we find ourselves in trouble or danger. His strength is always there, of course, and ever available to His children. But if we've allowed clutter to build up in our relationship with God, if we've allowed that living, pulsing sense of His reality in our lives to fade, our faith may be very small at just the time when we need faith the most.

A friend once told me about a small boy in Oklahoma named Billy, who had Down's syndrome. One day Billy visited a little church in town with the pastor's son, who had befriended him. When the pastor said, "Is there anyone here who wants to give his or her life to Jesus?" Billy immediately lifted his hand.

From that time on, Billy came every Sunday, choosing pew number two as his designated spot. And if you happened to get there first and sit down in that pew, he'd sit right in your lap.

Sometimes, during worship, God would move on Billy's heart, and he would lift his hands, tears filling his eyes and spilling down his cheeks. Five minutes or so later, God would move on others in the congregation. It always seemed that when God began to touch people's hearts in that little church, Billy was the first one to sense His presence. Others would follow after.

After telling me that story, my friend speculated that Billy didn't have a lot of clutter in his life. When the Holy Spirit began to touch people, Billy was wide open; nothing hindered his response.

Why is it so difficult for us to hear from God sometimes? Because our lives are so often cluttered with cares and worries and preoccupations and noise that God can't get through to us. But Billy was a simple young man, and the Lord had immediate access to his heart.

In the book of Hebrews we find this strong invitation:

> *Let us therefore come boldly to the throne of grace,*
> *that we may obtain mercy and find grace to help*
> *in time of need. (Hebrews 4:16)*

I think there are a couple of ways to look at this verse. Yes, I can certainly run to the throne of grace when I'm in trouble and it's a time of need. But in an ever deeper sense I hear this verse saying, "Why don't you walk and talk with God every day and store up some grace and mercy? Then, in the time of your great trouble and fear, you will already know and be experiencing the grip of His strong hand."

Life is unpredictable. Challenges are unavoidable. I see this verse urging us to come boldly again and again to the throne of grace, keeping our mercy-and-grace tank full, *because we never know when we will desperately need it.*

I'll let you in on a little secret. The older I get, the more I just want to *live* at His throne of grace and mercy. I want to pitch my tent and set up camp right there. I want to spend my life in that place. I may be preaching or counseling or writing or spending time with my family, but I want to keep at least one foot—one part of my heart and soul—before that throne where the grace flows. I want to live with a deep, abiding confidence in God, because I know Him and He knows me, and I'm no stranger to His courts. I want to be able to look the enemy in the eye and say, "I know who and what I am dealing with, and I know my God is greater than anything you can throw at me. I've been to the throne of grace before, and I am well acquainted with His mercy and power."

I've learned that confidence in God always brings courage before our enemy.

From *A Prayer That Moves Heaven,* Chapter 2

ASK

"Ask, and it will be given to you;
seek, and you will find; knock, and it will be opened to you.
For everyone who asks receives, and he who seeks finds,
and to him who knocks it will be opened."

MATTHEW 7:7-8

"And whatever you ask in My name, that I will do,
that the Father may be glorified in the Son."

JOHN 14:13

Be anxious for nothing, but in everything by prayer and
supplication, with thanksgiving, let your requests be made known to
God; and the peace of God, which surpasses all understanding,
will guard your hearts and minds through Christ Jesus.

PHILIPPIANS 4:6-7

CHAPTER 5

SO WHY NOT ASK?

BRUCE WILKINSON

⚘

"Oh, that you would bless me indeed!"

1 CHRONICLES 4:10

You're at a spiritual retreat in the mountains with others who want to experience a fuller Christian life. For the duration of the retreat everyone has been matched with a mentor. Yours is in his seventies, and he's been touching lives for God longer than you've been alive.

On the way to the showers the first morning, you walk past his room. His door is ajar, and he has just knelt down to pray. You can't resist. *How exactly does a giant of the faith begin his prayers?* you wonder.

You pause and lean closer. *Will he pray for revival? Pray for the hungry around the world? Pray for you?*

But this is what you hear: "O Lord, I beg you first and most this morning, please bless...*me!*"

Startled at such a selfish prayer, you pad down the hall to your shower. But as you're adjusting the water temperature, a thought hits you. It's so obvious, you can't believe you haven't thought it before:

Great men of the faith think differently than the rest of us.

By the time you're dressed and heading for breakfast, you're sure of it. The reason some men and women of faith rise above the rest, you decide, is that they think and pray differently than those around them.

Is it possible that God wants you to be "selfish" in your prayers? To ask for more—and more again—from your Lord? I've met so many earnest Christians who take it as a sign of immaturity to think such thoughts. They assume they'll seem impolite or greedy if they ask God for too many blessings.

Maybe you think like that. If you do, I want to show you that such a prayer is not the self-centered act it might appear, but a supremely spiritual one and exactly the kind of request our Father longs to hear.

First, let's take a closer look at Jabez's story.

NOT PAIN, BUT GAIN

As far as we can tell, Jabez lived in southern Israel after the conquest of Canaan and during the time of the judges. He was born into the tribe of Judah and eventually became the notable head of a clan. Yet his story really begins with his name: "His mother called his name Jabez, saying, 'Because I bore him in pain.'"

In Hebrew, the word *Jabez* means "pain." A literal rendering could read, "He causes (or will cause) pain."

Doesn't sound like the start of a promising life, does it? All babies arrive with a certain amount of pain, but something about Jabez's birth went beyond the usual—so much so that his mother chose to memorialize it in her son's name. Why? The pregnancy or the delivery may have been traumatic. Perhaps the baby was born breech. Or perhaps the mother's pain was emotional—maybe the child's father abandoned her during the pregnancy; maybe he had died; maybe the family had fallen into such financial straits that the prospect of another mouth to feed brought only fear and worry.

Only God knows for sure what caused the pain of this anguished mother. Not that it made much difference to young Jabez. He grew up with a name any boy would love to hate. Imagine if you had to go through childhood enduring the teasing of bullies, the daily reminders of your unwelcome arrival, and mocking questions like, "So, young man, what *was* your mother thinking?"

Yet by far the heaviest burden of Jabez's name was how it defined his future. In Bible times, a man and his name were so intimately related that "to cut off the name" of an individual amounted to the same thing as killing him. A name was often taken as a wish for or prophecy about the child's future. For example, Jacob can mean "grabber," a good one-word biography for that scheming patriarch. Naomi and her husband named their two sons Mahlon and Chilion. Translation? "Puny" and "pining." And that was exactly what they were. Both of them died in early adulthood. Solomon means "peace," and sure enough, he became the first king of Israel to reign without going to war. A name that meant "pain" didn't bode well for Jabez's future.

Despite his dismal prospects, Jabez found a way out. He had grown up hearing about the God of Israel who had freed his forefathers from slavery, rescued them from powerful enemies, and established them in a land of plenty. By the time he was an adult, Jabez believed and fervently hoped in this God of miracles and new beginnings. So why not ask for one? That's what he did. He prayed the biggest, most improbable request imaginable.

"Oh, that You would bless me *indeed…*!"

I love the urgency, the personal vulnerability of his plea. In Hebrew, adding "indeed" to this prayer was like adding five exclamation points, or writing the request in capital letters and underlining it.

In my mind's eye, I picture Jabez standing before a massive gate recessed into a sky-high wall. Weighted down by the sorrow of his past and the dreariness of his present, he sees before him only impossibility—a future shut off. But raising his hands to heaven, he cries out, "Father, oh, Father! Please bless me! And what I really mean is…bless me a lot!"

With the last word, the transformation begins. He hears a tremendous crack. Then a groan. Then a rumble as the huge gate swings away from him in a wide arc. There, stretching to the horizon, are fields of blessings.

And Jabez steps forward into another life.

Blessing Is Not About Sneezing

Before we can ask for God's blessing with confidence, we need a clear understanding of what the word means. We hear "bless" or "blessing" intoned from every pulpit. We ask God to bless the missionaries, the kids, and the food we're about to eat. It's something Grandma says when she hears you sneeze.

No wonder the meaning of blessing gets watered down to something vague and innocuous like "Have a nice day." No wonder so many Christians aren't as desperate as Jabez was to receive it!

To bless in the biblical sense means to ask for or to impart supernatural favor. When we ask for God's blessing, we're not asking for more of what we could get for ourselves. We're crying out for the wonderful, unlimited goodness that only God has the power to know about or give to us. This kind of richness is what the writer was referring to in Proverbs: "The Lord's bless-ing is our greatest wealth; all our work adds nothing to it" (Proverbs 10:22).

Notice a radical aspect of Jabez's request for blessing: *He left it entirely up to God to decide what the blessings would be and where, when, and how Jabez would receive them.* This kind of radical trust in God's good intentions toward us has nothing in common with the popular gospel that you should ask God for a Cadillac, a six-figure income, or some other material sign that you have found a way to cash in on your connection with Him. Instead, the Jabez blessing focuses like a laser on our wanting for ourselves nothing more and nothing less than what God wants for us.

When we seek God's blessing as the ultimate value in life, we are throwing ourselves entirely into the river of His will and power and purposes for us. All our other needs become second-ary to what we really want—which is to become wholly immersed in what God is trying to do in us, through us, and around us for His glory.

Let me tell you a guaranteed byproduct of sincerely seeking His blessing: Your life will become marked by miracles. How do I know? Because He promises it, and I've seen it happen in my own! God's power to accomplish great things suddenly finds no obstruction in you. You're moving in His direction. You're praying for exactly what god desires. Suddenly the unhindered forces of heaven can begin to accomplish God's perfect will—through you. And you will be the first to notice!

But there's a catch.

MR. JONES GOES TO HEAVEN

What if you found out that God had it in mind to send you twenty-three specific blessings today, but you got only one? What do you suppose the reason would be?

There's a little fable about a Mr. Jones who dies and goes to heaven. Peter is waiting at the gates to give him a tour. Amid the splendor of golden streets, beautiful mansions, and choirs of angels that Peter shows him, Mr. Jones notices an odd-looking building. He thinks it looks like an enormous warehouse—it has no windows and only one door. But when he asks to see inside, Peter hesitates. "You really don't want to see what's in there," he tells the new arrival.

Why would there be any secrets in heaven? Jones wonders. *What incredible surprise could be waiting for me in there?* When the official tour is over he's still wondering, so he asks again to see inside the structure.

Finally Peter relents. When the apostle opens the door, Mr. Jones almost knocks him over in his haste to enter. It turns out that the enormous building is filled with row after row of shelves, floor to ceiling, each stacked neatly with white boxes tied in red ribbons.

"These boxes all have names on them," Mr. Jones muses aloud.

Then turning to Peter he asks, "Do I have one?"

"Yes, you do." Peter tries to guide Mr. Jones back outside.

"Frankly," Peter says, "if I were you…." But Mr. Jones is already dashing toward the "J" aisle to find his box. Peter follows, shaking his head. He catches up with Mr. Jones just as he is slipping the red ribbon off his box and popping the lid. Looking inside, Jones has a moment of instant recognition, and he lets out a deep sigh like the ones Peter has heard so many times before.

Because there in Mr. Jones's white box are all the blessings that God wanted to give to him while he was on earth…but Mr. Jones had never asked.

"Ask," promised Jesus, "and it will be given to you" (Matthew 7:7). "You do not have because you do not ask," said James (James 4:2). Even though there is not limit to God's goodness, if you didn't ask Him for a blessing yesterday, you didn't get all that you were supposed to have.

That's the catch—if you don't ask for His blessing, you forfeit those that come to you only when you ask. In the same way that a father is honored to have a child beg for his blessing, your Father is delighted to respond generously when His blessing is what you covet most.

God's Nature Is to Bless

Perhaps you think that your name is just another word for pain or trouble, or that the legacy you have been handed from your family circumstances is nothing but a liability. You just don't feel like a candidate for blessing.

Or perhaps you're one of those Christians who thinks that once you're saved, God's blessings sort of drizzle over your life at a predetermined rate, no matter what you do. No extra effort required.

Or perhaps you have slipped into a ledger-keeping mind-set with God. In your blessing account you have a column for deposits and one for withdrawals. Has God been unusually kind to you lately? Then you think that you shouldn't expect, much less ask for, Him to credit your account. You might even think He should ignore you for a while, or even debit your account by sending some trouble your way.

This kind of thinking is a sin and a trap! When Moses said to God on Mount Sinai, "Show me Your glory," (Exodus 33:18), he was asking for a more intimate understanding of God. In response, God described Himself as "the Lord, the Lord God, merciful and gracious, longsuffering, and abounding in goodness and truth" (34:6).

Incredible! The very nature of God is to have goodness in so much abundance that it overflows into our unworthy lives.

If you think about God in any other way than that, I'm asking you to change the way you think. Why not make it a lifelong commitment to ask God every day to bless you—and while He's at it, bless you *a lot?*

God's bounty is limited only by us, not by His resources, power, or willingness to give. Jabez was blessed simply because he refused to let any obstacle, person, or opinion loom larger than God's nature. And God's nature is to bless.

His kindness in recording Jabez's story in the Bible is proof that it's not who you are, or what your parents decided for you, or what you were "fated" to be that counts. What counts is knowing who you want to be and asking for it.

Through a simple, believing prayer, you can change your future. You can change what happens one minute from now.

From *The Prayer of Jabez,* Chapter 2

Chapter 6

For the Asking

David Jeremiah

᪗

Once when my wife and I were traveling and had gone out to dinner with some friends, my cell phone rang in the middle of our meal. I answered it, and it was our grandson, David Todd, who was four years old at the time.

"Poppy," he said, "where are you?"

I told him where we were.

"Poppy," he said, "could you bring home the shopping mall magazine from the airplane?"

Now that wasn't exactly a request I might have anticipated. But it happened to be a major concern at the time to David Todd.

I found out later (when his dad got on the phone) that on a long airplane flight home with his mother, my grandson had discovered that little magazine in the seat pocket of the airplane that shows pictures of all those wonderful and interesting products. (I think he's inherited some shopping genes from his grandmother.)

He started paging through the magazine and looking at all those things, and then got excited to learn that when the flight was over he could actually take the magazine home with him.

However, he went to sleep during the flight, and when the plane landed and they got off, he forgot the magazine. When he remembered it too late, he was quite disappointed.

So I promised my grandson that I would bring him a copy of that magazine on our way home. He had asked me for it, and that's all he had to do. Why? Because he's my grandson, and anything he requests from me—if it's within my power, and it isn't harmful for him—I'm going to do for him.

I've learned in recent years that that's exactly how God is in His view toward us as we make our requests to Him. But this wasn't the perspective I always held on the matter.

Breaking Down God's Reluctance?

Before I first entered the hospital years ago for cancer treatment, I had the idea in the back of my mind that prayer was breaking down God's reluctance to do something for us. Maybe it was just my previous lack of attention to the Word of God or to those who taught it, but for some reason, this was my underlying attitude about it.

I don't mean that this thought was always consciously in mind whenever I prayed. Nor am I saying I no longer believe we should practice importunity and perseverance in how we pray.

But I've modified my thinking a little about all this, and what I've learned has changed my life. I've discovered that God is in no way dragging His feet about providing what we need. He isn't in heaven calculating whether we've done everything perfectly right so He can in turn do something good for us. Instead, He's waiting and more than willing to provide everything we require.

As He watches over you and me, I don't think He's sitting up in heaven thinking, *If they'll just ask enough times, I'll grant their request.* I think rather that He's in heaven wondering primarily why we don't ask more often.

So where did we get that idea that prayer is breaking down God's reluctance? Why do we tend to think we have to bash in the door of God's unwillingness?

The Bible doesn't teach that view. In fact, the Bible teaches just the opposite about God: He "gives to all liberally and without reproach" (James 1:5). When we're in need, it isn't because of God's reluctance to meet those needs, but because of our reluctance to ask: "You do not have because you do not ask" (James 4:2).

If we ask God for something that's good, and God sees that it's good for us, He'll give it to us, and we'll be able to joyfully affirm with James, "Every good gift and every perfect gift is from above, and comes down from the Father of lights" (James 1:17).

Yet we often don't receive these good and perfect gifts that God so keenly wants to give us, because we simply don't ask for them.

An Open Door

There's a God in heaven who loves me more than I can ever know, and who's just waiting for me to come to Him with the needs and requests that are on my heart. And I'm especially reminded of that whenever I read the wonderful words Jesus said about prayer in Matthew 7.

They come near the end of His Sermon on the Mount. Remember what Jesus said there about asking and seeking and knocking?

> *"Ask, and it will be given to you; seek, and you will find; knock, and it will be opened to you. For everyone who asks receives, and he who seeks finds, and to him who knocks it will be opened. Or what man is there among you who, if his son asks for bread, will give him a stone? Or if he asks for a fish, will he give him a serpent? If you then, being evil, know how to give good gifts to your children, how much more will your Father who is in heaven give good things to those who ask Him!"* (Matthew 7:7–11)

You've more than likely read those words before. But how fully and completely has it dawned upon you that almighty God, as your loving Father, is eagerly waiting to give you anything and everything you need and request? He has given us, in essence, an open door into His almighty presence and into His infinite storehouse of riches and blessings—for He "is able to do exceedingly abundantly above all that we ask" (Ephesians 3:20).

ENTICEMENT

In this passage in Matthew, these three little words *ask* and *seek* and *knock* are all imperatives. They're commands from the Lord Jesus. He didn't say, "If you feel like asking, then ask." He didn't say, "If you get around to it, why don't you seek?" Or, "If you're in the mood, you may want to try knocking." No, Jesus was telling us, "This is My command to you: Ask, seek, and knock. If you want Me to act on your behalf, then that's how it works. My requirement is that you simply *ask.*"Whatever we need, we must ask for it. And when we don't, we're disobedient to Jesus.

You may sometimes think, *I probably shouldn't be wasting God's time by telling Him about my little problems.* Or, *I don't feel I have any right to ask Him, knowing what kind of person I am, and knowing who God is.* But the fact is, the Lord has commanded you to ask Him. Whatever your problems, whatever your needs, whatever difficulties you're experiencing, if you haven't asked God about them, you're disobedient.

But it's also much more than a matter of obedience or disobedience. Our Father in heaven *wants* to hear You express to Him all the things that you feel you truly want and need.

As I read the words of Jesus in that passage, I can't sniff even a particle of guilt anywhere in it (unlike some of the books I've read on prayer, those that seem to be little more than guilt-ridden tirades on why we don't pray and why we should pray more). Jesus doesn't want to goad us into praying as much He desires to entice us into it.

It's almost as if He says, "Come, partake of My banquet. It's free! Do you see the freshly baked bread piled high on one table? It's for you. Can you smell the delicious aroma of the roasted main course, the sweet fragrance of the pastries and pies and cakes, the wholesome fragrance of newly picked vegetables and fruits? It's all yours! I've provided all you need. I have enough for everyone, and there's no need to fear I'll run out of anything. I'm inviting you to My feast—your place at My table is reserved. All I require is that you *ask* My Father to give you what you need. That's it! That's the only thing lacking."

KEEP ON

Those three little words in Matthew 7:7 are not only imperatives, but in their original Greek tense they have a kind of continuing action connected with them. Jesus is saying *keep on* asking, *keep on* seeking, and *keep on* knocking. Don't ever stop; just keep doing it. Always, whatever you need—just ask.

We could learn a lot from children on that score, couldn't we? I remember hearing a story about a little boy who was at home with his father while the mother was away for the evening. The father (who wasn't as familiar with the boy's bedtime routine as the mother was) was trying to get the boy to sleep. Shortly after tucking his son into bed for the night, he was reading his newspaper when he heard a little voice calling out from the bedroom: "Daddy? I need a drink of water."

The father went upstairs and brought him a drink of water, and of course a short time later the boy called out to say he had to go to the bathroom. Repeatedly the boy kept calling his father to come up and take care of this or that—locating a lost teddy bear, turning on a night light, shutting a closet door.

Finally the exasperated dad reached the limit of his patience. "No more. Young man, you're fine, so get quiet! If I hear another sound from you, I'll come up and give you a spanking!"

For several moments, all was silent. Then the little voice drifted downstairs once more: "Daddy, when you come up here to spank me, could you bring me another drink of water?"

That's how children are. They never quit. It doesn't matter how many times you say no, they keep coming back. They keep asking. They ask and ask and ask.

A, S, K

These commands in Matthew 7:7 come in a certain kind of progression, with each one a little more intense than the one preceding it. *Ask* is strong enough, but *seek* is stronger, and *knock* is even more intense. Sometimes God wants us to turn up the heat in our prayers for something we're asking from Him.

But the basic thrust of the passage is simply that we're to *ask*. And just so we don't miss its importance, Jesus uses that little word a total of five times in this brief passage on prayer.

In case you're ever explaining this passage to your children or someone else, and they don't seem to be grasping the main point of what Jesus is saying, tell them you'll show it to them in a special code. Have them write down those three basic commands in Matthew 7:7 in a list:

A s k
S e e k
K n o c k

Then take a closer look at the first letters of each word in the list. And there you have it! Simple as that: Just *ask*!

First Resort

People often come to me, as a pastor, and ask for my advice on some opportunity or decision or difficulty they're facing.

Sometimes I'll say, "Have you asked God about it?" And more often than not the reply will be, "Well…no, I guess I haven't."

Let me tell you, asking God about it is always the best place to start, no matter what issue or opportunity you're facing. He needs to be our first resort, not our last. Why would anyone come to David Jeremiah before they approach the Creator of the universe? God has entire worlds in His back pocket; what do I have in comparison to that?

"We pray when there's nothing else we can do," writes Oswald Chambers, "but Jesus wants us to pray before we do anything at all."

So ask your Father in heaven for whatever it is you need. Ask for provision of your daily necessities. Ask for protection when you're threatened or afraid. Ask Him to show you the right priorities in how you spend your time and money and energy. Ask Him for special guidance when your circumstances call for it.

_____

From *The Prayer Matrix,* Chapter 1

CHAPTER 7

A Mother Who Wouldn't Give Up

GREG LAURIE

In Matthew 15, we find a reminder that those things we think are barriers from God are often, in reality, bridges to His greater blessings. The story told is that of a mother who wouldn't quit asking Jesus to heal her daughter, and it's a story that gives hope to all parents who care about the well-being of their children.

As the story begins, Jesus initially puts this woman off, as though He just doesn't have time for a non-Jew coming to Him for help. But another dynamic is at work. He isn't trying to destroy her faith; He is developing it. He isn't trying to make the situation more difficult; He is drawing her faith out. He knows she will overcome any barriers in her path because her faith is strong, and He wants to commend her.

We're told that this woman is a Canaanite, which means she probably is a worshiper of pagan deities. She may have become disillusioned with these false gods, because she comes seeking Jesus, the one true God. She has an accurate assessment of her own spiritual condition when she comes; she doesn't demand anything from the Lord, but instead cries for mercy, saying, "Have mercy on me, O Lord, Son of David! My daughter is severely demon-possessed" (Matthew 15:22).

This mother, like any good mother, cares desperately about the condition of her daughter, who has come under the power of demonic spirits. How the daughter ended up this way, we don't know. Perhaps her mother's pagan involvement up to that point has affected her daughter. Maybe there are many little idols and gods in the home, and these have opened a doorway to demonic power in this girl's life.

This is a reminder that actions and beliefs do have a direct influence on our children. We see it all too often in our society as crimes and sins are passed from generation to generation. For instance, statistics show that children of divorced parents are far more likely to end up divorcing as well. The same is true of alcoholism and other addictions. Only the power of God can break that cycle of sin.

A SERIES OF BARRIERS

This mother comes to Jesus with her heartfelt need, casting herself on His mercy. His reaction might lead us to believe that

Jesus was heartless and uncaring. But nothing could be further from the truth. What is in fact happening is that Jesus is testing the faith of this woman by setting up a series of barriers.

First, He is silent: "He answered her not a word" (verse 23). Sometimes the hardest response to accept is no response at all. But what appears to be a brush-off is actually an invitation for her to step in, to be persistent and not let go.

The disciples, however, interpret their Master's silence to mean He doesn't want to be bothered, especially since the woman is creating a bit of a scene. His disciples urge Him, saying, "Send her away, for she cries out after us" (15:23).

"Lord," they say, "get rid of this nagging lady." Jesus doesn't throw her out, but the way He responds doesn't exactly sound like an invitation for her to stick around either: "I was not sent except to the lost sheep of the house of Israel" (15:24).

Slam! The door is shut in this mother's face. But she just keeps knocking. She refuses to be discouraged in her quest.

So she comes and worships Him, saying, "Lord, help me!" (15:25).

But Jesus isn't through testing her perseverance. He answers, "It is not good to take the children's bread and throw it to the little dogs" (15:26).

Dogs? Not exactly a compliment. Maybe now this woman will give up her hopeless quest! But when Christ calls her a dog, she just picks up what He says and brings it back to Him—like a faithful hound picking up the master's stick and dropping it at his feet.

She says, "Yes, Lord, yet even the little dogs eat the crumbs which fall from their masters' table" (15:27).

I think a smile crosses the face of Jesus at that moment. The woman's faith is so great that she knows even a tiny leftover of Jesus' power will be enough to heal her daughter.

Jesus has heard what He wanted to hear. Now He dramatically changes His manner with her. He says, "O woman, great is your faith! Let it be to you as you desire" (15:28).

The mouths of the disciples drop open at this. All this time they thought Jesus was brushing her off, clearly stamping her request with a NO. Then suddenly He turns around and tells the Canaanite woman essentially that she can have whatever she wants! He is giving her carte blanche. What a statement! *Let it be as you desire.*

What she desires, of course, is her daughter's freedom from a devilish influence in her life—and she gets it. In fact, her daughter is healed "that very hour" (15:28).

So what qualified this woman to have such a thing said to her? What brought her to a place where Jesus would offer her such an incredible privilege?

Above all, I think it had to be her persistence, her tenacity, her commitment. This is the kind of faith *we* need. When we're praying for something we believe is in accordance with the will of God, we should not give up. If at first you don't succeed, keep asking, keep seeking, and keep knocking.

PASSIONATE AND PERSISTENT

Remember the story Jesus told of the friend who came at midnight to pound on his neighbor's door and ask for bread? It was late and the man and his family were asleep, for crying out loud! This was no time for getting up to gather a few loaves of bread. But Jesus makes this point:

> *I say to you, though he will not rise and give to him because he is his friend, yet because of his persistence he will rise and give him as many as he needs. (Luke 11:8)*

Then our Lord tells us, "So I say to you, ask, and it will be given to you; seek, and you will find; knock, and it will be opened to you. For everyone who asks receives, and he who seeks finds, and to him who knocks it will be opened" (11:9–10).

Often in prayer we will ask God for something once or twice, then give up. But God doesn't want us to take His silence for a final answer; instead we are to ask, seek, and knock.

Jesus' language in this verse is unusually compelling, because these three verbs indicate an ascending order of intensity.

"Ask" implies our request for assistance. We realize our need and ask for help. The word implies that we are to be humble in submitting our request.

"Seek" also denotes asking but adds the aspect of *action*. We don't just express our need, but we get up and look around for help. This involves effort—the prayerful effort of searching for God's answers, especially in His Word!

"Knock" includes asking, taking action, *and* the aspect of *persevering*—like the neighbor pounding on his friend's door at midnight.

So the stacking of these words is extremely forceful, as is the Greek verb tense used. The literal meaning is this: *"Keep on asking and it will be given to you, keep on seeking and you will find it, keep on knocking and the door will be opened."*

Jesus is calling us to passionate, persistent prayer!

STALKING THE JUDGE

When Jesus said that we "ought always to pray and not lose heart," He told another vivid story to get across that concept to His disciples.

> *There was in a certain city a judge who did not fear God nor regard man. Now there was a widow in that city; and she came to him, saying, "Get justice for me from my adversary." (Luke 18:1–3)*

This judge would likely be one of the men appointed to such positions by the Romans or by King Herod—men who were notorious for their corruption.

The person bringing a plea before this judge was first of all a woman, meaning she had little standing in the culture of that time. Moreover, she was a widow, having no husband to be her advocate in court. With no husband she was also probably poor, with no money to offer the judge a bribe. She had nothing to fall back on except Persistence with a capital P.

At first the judge paid her no attention, but then he gets to thinking.

> But afterward he said within himself, "Though I
> do not fear God nor regard man, yet because this
> widow troubles me I will avenge her, lest by her
> continual coming she weary me." (18:4–5)

In other words, this woman was driving him crazy. The Greek word used here for "troubling" him is very suggestive—the image it gives is of beating someone black and blue, or giving them a black eye. Essentially this judge was thinking, *If I don't give this woman what she wants, she's going to beat me senseless!* It almost sounds as if she was stalking the judge. No wonder he decided to give her what she wanted.

So what's the point? Should we threaten God? Do we need to bully Him to get Him to do what we want?

Look at the lesson Jesus teaches:

> *And shall God not avenge His own elect who cry out day and night to Him, though He bears long with them? I tell you that He will avenge them speedily. Nevertheless, when the Son of Man comes, will He really find faith on the earth? (18:6–8)*

If a poor widow got what she deserved from a selfish judge, how much more will God's children receive what is right from their loving heavenly Father!

Think with me now about the differences between the widow's situation and our own:

1. *This woman was a stranger to the judge, but we come before God as His children.*

2. *This widow had no guaranteed access to the judge, but God's children have open access to him 24-7. At any time, "we can boldly enter heaven's Most Holy Place because of the blood of Jesus" (Hebrews 10:19). "Let us therefore come boldly to the throne of grace, that we*

*may obtain mercy and find grace to help in
time of need" (Hebrews 4:16).*

3. *This woman had no friend at court to plead
her case, no husband or attorney to stand up
and defend her—no inside connection at all.
All she could do was walk around the outside
of the judge's quarters and shout threats!
By contrast, "we have an Advocate with the
Father, Jesus Christ the righteous" (1 John 2:1).
We always have an attorney before God—and
He's the Son of the Judge!*

Not only that, but we also have the Holy Spirit teaching
us how to pray and taking hold of us in our prayers—energizing and directing our prayers—so that they're delivered through
Jesus Christ before a loving heavenly Father who so eagerly
wants to answer you and bless you!

That's why the Lord wants you to keep on praying and not
lose heart.

WHATEVER YOU WANT

Remember how Jesus at last responded to that Canaanite woman
with the stricken daughter. What would it take for God to come
to you right now and say, "I will give you whatever you want, no

limits—you name it and it's yours"? Have you shown the kind of full-of-faith perseverance that He wants to reward like that?

Maybe you, like this woman, know what it's like to have a child who's under the devil's influence. He or she has rejected your influence and God's influence, at least for now. Don't give up and don't feel like the Lord has abandoned you or failed you. Keep praying. Your children can escape your presence, but they cannot escape your prayers.

As you pray, make it your goal to find out the will of God and pray accordingly. Prayer isn't getting your way in heaven; it's getting God's way on earth.

What do you really want today? Salvation for your child? For your husband? For your friend? Then don't give up praying for them.

Or maybe it's not your child in trouble, but you. You've reached rock bottom yourself. Don't be embarrassed to come to the Lord with your problems and ask for His assistance. Call out to Him. Don't be discouraged. He's ready to help you and forgive you and to start changing you.

Don't let the devil whisper into your ear that it's too late—or worse, that God doesn't care. Remember that what may look like indifference on God's part may actually be a barrier that He wants you to overcome by persistent, faithful wrestling in prayer.

Keep praying!

The prayer that prevails with God is the one that we put our whole soul into, stretching out toward Him in intense and agonizing desire.

For God long ago promised that His people will find Him when they search for Him with all their heart (see Jeremiah 29:13).

From *Wrestling with God,* Chapter 3

CHAPTER 8

EXPRESSING YOUR NEEDS TO HIM

SHIRLEY DOBSON

⊰৯

Of all the aspects of prayer, "ask" is probably the one with which we can most easily identify. Who hasn't asked for something from our heavenly Father?

The truth is, we are remiss if we *don't* take our requests to the Lord. Jesus Himself taught us to pray, "Give us today our daily bread." But our Father encourages us to seek more than care of our physical needs. He wants to hear and meet our requests for spiritual and emotional fulfillment, too.

I remember a night when the Lord answered one of my urgent requests in a most tangible way. The kids, then quite young, and I were alone in our home; Jim was traveling. I was sleeping peacefully until suddenly, about 2 a.m., I awoke with a start. I didn't know why, but I was filled with fear!

I lay in bed for several minutes (it seemed like hours) and worried. Finally, I forced myself out of bed and sank to my knees.

"Oh, Lord," I prayed, "I don't know why I'm so frightened. I ask You to watch over our home and protect our family. Send Your guardian angel to be with us." I climbed back into bed. The fear had subsided somewhat, and a half hour later I was asleep. But in the morning a neighbor came over and said that a thief had broken into our next-door neighbor's home. The police had determined that the burglary occurred at 2 a.m.—the same time I had awakened in fear!

"If a burglar wanted to break into *our* house," I said, "he'd probably try to get in through the bathroom window near our children's bedrooms. Let's go look."

We checked that side of the house and saw that the window screen was bent and the windowsill splintered. Someone had indeed started to break in. But what had stopped him?

I'm convinced that the Lord protected us that night through my anxious prayer. God not only answered my plea in a literal sense by stopping evil at the gate, but He also gave me the peace I needed to go back to sleep and leave matters entirely in His hands.

Peter says, "Cast all your anxiety on him because he cares for you" (1 Peter 5:7). Our heavenly Father does care for us and desires to meet our needs. But for our own good—for the development of our active, healthy dependence on Him—He invites us to *ask* Him for these needs to be met. According to James, "You do not have, because you do not ask God" (James 4:2).

God makes prayer as easy as possible for us. He's completely approachable and available, and He'll never mock or upbraid us for bringing our needs before Him.

All He asks is that we make our requests known to Him.

GUIDELINES FOR ASKING

God tells us a great deal in Scripture about how to bring our requests before Him. This is obviously something He wants us to do often, for His own pleasure as well as for our well-being.

Ask in Jesus' name.

Jesus told His disciples, "Until now you have not asked for anything in my name. Ask and you will receive, and your joy will be complete" (John 16:24).

Asking in the name of another means that someone else has granted you the authority to submit a request in his name. More specifically, this person wants you to make a petition on his behalf. So, by asking in Jesus' name, we're making a request not only in His authority, but also for *His* interests and *His* benefit. Understanding this should revolutionize our commitment to prayer!

Praying in the name of Jesus also means coming to God on the merits of Christ rather than on our own qualifications. We're not worthy of even a moment of the Lord's time or attention, but Christ has infinite worth in His Father's eyes. Opening a prayer in Jesus' name is like visiting a powerful king and presenting a letter of introduction from an especially important nobleman; this letter allows you an unlimited claim to the king's attention and unrestricted access to his kingdom.

Ask while abiding in Jesus.

Jesus gave His disciples the image of a vine and its branches as a picture of His relationship to them (see John 15:1–6). He then said, "If you abide in Me, and My words abide in you, you will *ask what you desire,* and it shall be done for you" (v. 7).

As a child, I was introduced to Jesus by Mrs. Baldwin, the Sunday school teacher in my little neighborhood church. She described Him as my special friend, and thereafter I sought a closer relationship with Him. I began praying about the struggles inherent to living with an alcoholic father. I asked for a change in my father—and if he wouldn't change, I prayed that God would protect our family and give us a father who would love and take care of us.

My family disintegrated when I was in the sixth grade. My parents divorced, and we moved to a tiny "shoebox" of a house. But the Lord had not forgotten the prayer of a hopeful little girl. My mother soon met and married a wonderful man who became a devoted father, faithful husband, and good provider. They are now in their nineties and have lived together harmoniously for more than fifty years. This was the first of countless prayers that the Lord has answered decisively on my behalf.

From my first introduction to Jesus as a little girl, my relationship with Him grew steadily—as did my commitment to prayer. I believe that a fruitful prayer life begins with a total abiding in Christ, an alive and flourishing union with Him.

Ask according to God's will.

Jesus teaches this emphasis in His model prayer from Matthew 6:10: "Your will be done on earth as it is in heaven." The apostle Paul tells us that the will of God is "good, pleasing and perfect" (Romans 12:2). We must keep God's perfect will in focus as we make our requests.

Following this guideline doesn't restrict our asking; instead, it builds our confidence in prayer. "This is the confidence we have in approaching God," the apostle John writes, "that if we ask anything according to his will, he hears us. And if we know that he hears us—whatever we ask—we know that we have what we asked of him" (1 John 5:14–15).

We approach God, we ask within His will, and we *know* that He hears. This is our wondrous privilege as God's children!

Ask in faith.

We can clearly see the requirement to have *faith* in the instruction James gives us for requesting wisdom:

> *If any of you lacks wisdom, he should ask God,*
> *who gives generously to all without finding fault,*
> *and it will be given to him. But when he asks,*
> *he must believe and not doubt, because he who*
> *doubts is like a wave of the sea, blown and tossed*
> *by the wind. That man should not think he will*
> *receive anything from the Lord. (James 1:5–7)*

The certainty of answered prayer comes through even more strongly in the words of Jesus. "Ask and it will be given to you; seek and you will find; knock and the door will be opened to you. For everyone who asks receives; he who seeks finds; and to him who knocks, the door will be opened" (Matthew 7:7–8).

When my children were young, I began praying and fasting for them on a weekly basis, a practice I continue to this day. I believe that over the years these prayers have protected them from many dangers, particularly during a six-month period when we almost lost one or the other on four separate occasions. There is *power* in faithful prayer. I would never have been able to keep up my commitment to pray and fast for my children if I didn't believe wholeheartedly in their effectiveness—and in the awesome authority of Almighty God.

Ask with thanksgiving.

"Do not be anxious about anything," Paul tells us, "but in everything, by prayer and petition, *with thanksgiving,* present your requests to God" (Philippians 4:6). This "thanksgiving" is the inevitable—and sometimes overwhelming—result of our faith in God's answers to our prayers, and our faith in God's loving control over every aspect of our lives.

Ask with right motives.

"When you ask," James tells us, "you do not receive, because you ask with wrong motives, that you may spend what you get on your pleasures" (James 4:3). If our prayers aren't answered the way we want, it doesn't necessarily mean that our motives are wrong—but we can be sure that asking God to stretch, bend, or manipulate His laws to fit our selfish desires or circumstances will lead to an unfavorable response.

THE SCOPE OF OUR REQUESTS

When the Holy Spirit comes to dwell within us, I believe we

gain a built-in inclination to take our concerns and needs to the Lord in prayer. Read again Paul's words from Philippians 4:6: "Do not be anxious about anything, but in *everything*...present your requests to God." *Nothing* qualifies for worry; *everything* qualifies for prayer.

By the same work of the Spirit within us, I believe we can learn to look beyond our personal situation to those around us—our families, our communities, our nation, and our world. God will instill His concern for others within our hearts so that we start to care for them as He does. Our prayers for them begin to flow more readily. We yearn for others to receive their salvation from His hand, to know His tender care as their Father and Friend.

This is one of the reasons for my involvement with the National Day of Prayer. I believe that this annual call to prayer is just one example of a way to extend our care and concern for all of God's children. As we open our hearts and prayers to God's leading, we join in His work around the world. This is what we were born for—or rather, *re*born for!

When we come before the Lord with praise, humbly repent of our transgressions, and in obedience present our petitions to God according to the guidelines set out for us in Scripture, He *will* answer. Our final task, then, is to yield to His perfect will.

———————

From *Certain Peace in Uncertain Times,* Chapter 5

WAIT

ॐ

Wait on the LORD; be of good courage,
and He shall strengthen your heart;
wait, I say, on the LORD!

PSALM 27:14

I waited patiently for the LORD;
and He inclined to me,
and heard my cry. He also brought
me up out of a horrible pit.

PSALM 40:1-2

"Behold, this is our God; we have waited for Him,
and He will save us. This is the LORD;
we have waited for Him;
we will be glad and rejoice in His salvation."

ISAIAH 25:9

CHAPTER 9

DAILY PRAYER OF EXPECTANCY

RUTH MYERS

᠅

Father in heaven, great and powerful and full of love,
I lift my heart in praise for the privilege of coming
to You in prayer. Give me special grace as I join
Your exalted Son in His ministry of prayer.
Search my heart, Lord, and show me if any sin is
hindering Your work in my life.
May I respond without delay whenever You make
me conscious of sin. How grateful I am for Your
total forgiveness the moment I confess my sin,
turning back to You as my Lord!
And Father, teach me to pray. How much I yearn to
know Your will and Your way. I thank You that
Your Son lives within me. What a joy to know
that He is my teacher—that through Him I can
learn to pray. I can learn to release Your boundless

power for both my needs and the needs of many
others, near and far. Teach me to pray.
Day by day may Your Spirit work in me, motivating
me to abide in Christ and pray in faith,
moving Your mighty hand to fulfill Your purposes.
Keep reminding me that You are able to do
infinitely more than I would ever dare to ask or
imagine, by Your mighty power at work within me.
To You be the glory both now and forever.
Amen.

———————————

From *31 Days of Prayer,* Introduction

CHAPTER 10

FREE FROM MY BEST
Prayer and God's Unlimited Blessing

OLIVER NORTH

꒪꒱

*How did I come to submit my neck to your easy yoke,
and allow my shoulders to carry your light burden? Instantly your
yoke and burden, dear Christ, felt wonderfully sweet,
so much sweeter than those vain delights which I had forsaken.
Indeed it was a joy to me to be deprived of those joys
which earlier I had feared to lose. For you, O Lord, cast them
away from me, and in their place you yourself entered me,
bringing joy which is sweeter than any earthly pleasure.*

AUGUSTINE OF HIPPO (354—430)

Having lived for three quarters of a century, Abram was comfortable and well established in the thriving Mesopotamian city of Ur. He was near his family and everything he had ever known.

His one significant disappointment was his and Sarai's childless-ness—a great disgrace in that culture. But he was doing his best.

Then God stepped in.

"Leave your country, your people and your father's house-hold and go to the land I will show you," God commanded (Genesis 12:1). Along with the command came God's promise of numerous descendants and great blessing through Abram on all nations of the world.

Bewildered but intrigued, Abram obeyed God and left his home. Throughout the rest of his life, as an alien wandering the land promised to him, he would take possession of only one small plot to use as a burial site for his wife.

Some years after he had arrived in God's Promised Land, Abram and Sarai were still unable to conceive. So Sarai, with Abram's consent, decided it was in their best interest to produce this promised offspring their own way. Abram slept with Sarai's servant Hagar, and she bore his first son, Ishmael, who became the ancestor of all the Arab nations.

But what Abram thought was best—to produce his own heir—fell far short of God's dream. One day God appeared to Abram and confirmed that His promise would be fulfilled through a son born to Sarai. To highlight this historic turning point, God changed their names to Abraham and Sarah. True to God's promise, Isaac was born one year later, to Abraham, age one hundred, and Sarah, ninety-one.

But God was not finished fulfilling His promises. We can now look back and see that it was through Abraham's son Isaac that God produced His chosen people, Israel. And it was through Israel that God brought His Son, Jesus the Messiah, into the world to live and to die on our behalf. Not only did Abraham become the physical father of all Israel, but he also became the spiritual father of all who would trust Christ with the same faith Abraham expressed toward God (Romans 4:16–17).

This nomadic patriarch, who would otherwise have disappeared into obscurity, became known as "God's friend" (James 2:23). Because Abraham desired above all else to walk closely with God, God responded by doing far more than Abraham could have dreamed. He used this man as His instrument for carrying out His worldwide, millennia-spanning plan for the salvation of billions and for the establishment of His kingdom on earth.

OUR BEST VERSUS GOD'S BEST

We humans are limited beings. That's not a bad thing. It's a simple fact of God's wise design. We don't know everything, so we need His guidance. We can't do everything, so we need His power. We can't love perfectly, so we need His heart.

During my younger years I failed to grasp how limited my vision was. To me, "the best" meant becoming the bravest marine and the sharpest officer the Corps had ever seen. And doing it on my own. My best was to save South Vietnam—to lead the men who would preserve freedom in yet another region of the globe.

These were good desires, but in my myopia, I was cutting myself off from the much greater good God wanted to lavish on me. I didn't have to stop being a marine or stop contributing to freedom in the world, but God had another mission at home that only I could carry out. There was a woman He commanded me to love and care for, and there were growing children who needed their father's time. I thank God that He broadened my perspective to see the bigger picture. If I had neglected my family, little else I would have done in my life would have amounted to much in heaven's ledgers.

God is the one who "is able to do immeasurably more than all we ask or imagine, according to his power that is at work within us" (Ephesians 3:20).

It's as though we live in the bottom of a ditch. As long as we stay there, our horizons are radically constricted. If we don't know any better, we naturally think the inside of the ditch is all there is to our world...the best there is.

When I pray, God responds by lifting me up, allowing me to see beyond my constricted horizons into the infinitely wide vistas of His reality. Prayer opens the way for God to work out *His* dream for my life, to provide *His* resources for my fulfillment, to pour *His* unlimited blessings into my life and heart.

God can even teach us this lesson through our kids' toys. Syd's son Nathan has been a Legomaniac all his life—he still is today, as a married adult. One Christmas Nathan wanted a particular Lego set that contained some specialized pieces. Now, you have to understand that Nathan's wasn't just an if-you-get-around-to-it kind of request. It was one of those drop-a-hint-every-day-since-Thanksgiving requests.

But Syd didn't give Nathan what he asked for.

Syd did his homework and discovered a different set containing the same special pieces, but three times as large. He bought it and wrapped it for the big day. Though Nathan was adamant about the "best" gift Syd could give him, to Nathan's delight Syd surpassed it on Christmas morning.

To this day, when Syd is conscious that God might have far more to give than Syd's imagination allows him to ask, he says, "God, this is a Lego prayer. Please answer according to the abundance of Your riches." Here is a man who knows what he doesn't know.

PRAYING FOR GOD'S BEST

So what is God's best for each of us? That varies from person to person. Talk to God, and, in His time, He will help you discover His perfect plan for your life.

I do, however, know a few principles that might help you recognize and seek His best when you see it.

First, *God's best always begins and ends with Himself.* This is the discovery Augustine voiced in the prayer quoted at the beginning of this chapter. And we've already heard the psalmist's heart: "Whom have I in heaven but you? And earth has nothing I desire besides you" (Psalm 73:25). Finding and knowing God is what prayer is all about.

Second, *God's best always involves our obedience.* Notice, for example, that Jesus' promise of abundant blessing begins with a command: "Give, and it will be given to you. A good measure, pressed down, shaken together and running over, will be poured into your lap" (Luke 6:38). As you pray for God's best, offer yourself as His servant.

Third, *God gives His best to those who ask for it—and ask with pure motives.* "You do not have, because you do not ask God. When you ask, you do not receive, because you ask with wrong motives, that you may spend what you get on your pleasures" (James 4:2–3). God is so gracious that He gives blessing even to those who don't ask. But He reserves His best for those who do.

And fourth, *God's best is not always pain free.* In fact, sometimes God's best comes *through* pain. Peter explained that God allows suffering and hardship "so that your faith—of greater worth than gold, which perishes even though refined by fire— may be proved genuine and may result in praise, glory and honor when Jesus Christ is revealed" (1 Peter 1:7). Even Jesus, who never sinned, "learned obedience from what he suffered," and thereby became perfectly prepared to do His saving work (Hebrews 5:8; see also 2:10; 5:7–9).

When we pray about our pain—whether it's ahead of us, behind us, or right on top of us—God may not show us His reasons, but He assures us that He is in control and that He has a wise and loving purpose for everything. This kind of insight sustained my family and me through five long and difficult years of congressional hearings and criminal trials. During that time I was often reminded of a picture in my marine friend's office. It shows a raft riding through rough rapids, and the caption reads: "God doesn't promise you a smooth passage—just a safe delivery."

When Pain Is Best

Pain was instrumental in the life of the seventeenth-century mathematician and philosopher Blaise Pascal. Pascal lived only thirty-nine years, but in this short time he left an intellectual and spiritual legacy that has impacted the entire Western world. He was plagued by debilitating illness from age twenty-four on, and during one particularly difficult period near the end of his life he wrote a prayer, "On the Good Use of Sickness." The prayer, which in at least one English edition fills seven pages, begins:

O Lord, whose Spirit is so good and gracious in all things, and who is so merciful that not only prosperities but even the adversities that happen to your elect are the effects of your mercy, give me grace not to act like the unbelievers in the state you bring me into by your justice. Instead, like a true Christian, help me to acknowledge you as my Father and my God, in whatever circumstances you may place me. For no change of my circumstances can ever alter your will for my life. You are ever the same, though I may be subject to change. You are no less God when you are afflicting and punishing me than when you are consoling and showing compassion. *

Pascal understood that God's best was far beyond anything he could imagine and that God's method for fulfilling His good purpose in Pascal's life was not subject to Pascal's approval. He was willing to allow pain to do its work in his life because he knew God as his Father.

Pascal's attitude reflects that of the apostle John: "How great is the love the Father has lavished on us, that we should be called children of God! And that is what we are!" (1 John 3:1). When we draw close to God, we enjoy fresh amazement at the privilege of being His children, and we become better prepared to receive all the best He offers His kids. There's no way you can foresee the unlimited blessing your Father has in store for you. Pray, and you'll find it.

---

* James M. Houston, ed., *The Mind on Fire: An Anthology of the Writings of Blaise Pascal* (Portland, OR: Multnomah, 1989), 285.

From *True Freedom,* Chapter 7

CHAPTER 11

WAITING ON GOD

J. OTIS LEDBETTER

৩৯

I wait for the LORD, my soul waits,
and in His word I do hope.

PSALM 130:5

God waits in our secret place all the time, every day. He's never absent. To help us discover His will for us, He waits there for us to rendezvous with Him—something we're sometimes willing to do only after we've tried everything else.

And one of the things we often try is the "fleece" method of finding God's will, especially in understanding His timing for our planned actions. It's something I've used, and most everyone I've talked with about it has at one time or another "put out the fleece."

But is it a good way to go about finding God's leading? And if it isn't—why isn't it?

GIDEON'S EXPERIENCE

You remember the story.

Gideon, who was the least member of the least clan in his nation, was appointed by God to lead his people out from under the oppressive iron grip of the powerful Midianites.

As the decisive battle approached, Gideon longed for the confidence that God was indeed with Israel, and to make sure, he decided to use a simple fleece of wool. He laid it on the ground outside his tent, and made his request to the Lord—that in the morning, God would make the fleece wet and the ground around it dry.

The next morning, Gideon rose early. The ground was dry, but he squeezed a bowlful of dew from the fleece. God had honored his request.

Gideon then pleaded for yet another sign on the next night as well, again using the fleece: "Let it now be dry only on the fleece, but on all the ground let there be dew" (Judges 6:39).

The next morning, he discovered that God had again answered his request, and Gideon was satisfied.

SO TEMPTING

Obviously, the fleece worked well for Gideon. Down through the ages people have read his story, marveled at the simplicity of it, and tried to duplicate its success. It promises to take the guesswork out of discerning God's direction for our lives.

In my opinion, however, relying on a fleece is a dangerous mistake. It's an attempted shortcut for people who want instant results instead of being committed enough to develop a confident, personal understanding of God's will. When the Lord seems to be moving too slowly in guiding us, or His will doesn't seem clear, the fleece is such a tempting substitute for patience.

I've heard people testify that the fleece worked for them. But how do we really know it wasn't sheer coincidence or self-fulfilling prophecies? Or for that matter, how do we know it wasn't a set of circumstances orchestrated by the evil one?

RED DRESS, GREEN DRESS

Bobby was a young man I went to school with in Sherman, Texas. His athletic ability made him very popular. He came to the Lord after his senior year in high school and started attending the same church I did. His spiritual growth was impressive, and he followed the Lord as fiercely as he had pursued sports. He taught a children's class at church and also began reaching out to his former teammates, leading many to Christ. His passion for Jesus was so enthusiastic that many people in our church could easily envision the day Bobby would become a preacher.

One Sunday morning he gave a testimony about his future. He announced that he had surrendered to full-time Christian ministry, and applause broke out that lasted for what seemed like several minutes. But the enthusiasm of his audience quickly mellowed as Bobby went on with his story.

He told the church how hearing the sermon a few weeks earlier on Gideon and the fleece had inspired him to confirm a calling he'd sensed. "I wasn't sure if God really was asking me to do this or not," he admitted.

"Then Thursday morning I noticed a lady standing at the bus stop in front of my business wearing a red dress. I'd been wondering what God wanted me to do." Bobby paused, bowed his head, then raised his eyes as if looking out at us over invisible reading glasses. "So Thursday night during our family prayer time, I told God and my family that if He wanted me in ministry, to have a lady standing there at the bus stop in a green dress in the morning."

With his jaw squared, he quickly finished: "Sure enough, the next morning, there she stood in a green skirt. So here I am this morning, keeping my end of the bargain."

I knew Bobby personally. It wasn't my place to judge him, and he wasn't one to lie or fabricate a story. He seemed to truly trust the fleece for a while. But because the fleece was used as a shortcut around a clear, personal discernment of God's will, he later began to doubt the authenticity of his call.

Unfortunately the end of this story isn't a happy one. Bobby's ministry from that day forward was plagued with uncertainty, second guesses, and questions about what exactly God was doing. Finally he surrendered his calling altogether. He quit bringing people to church and grew embittered toward God. His entire spiritual life lay in ruin.

I heard Bobby complain one day that he wished God "would never have put that lady on that street corner that morning." Today, Bobby doesn't even attend church because he feels God betrayed him.

For whatever it's worth, I'm not sure God put that lady there. And, tragically, neither is Bobby.

Maybe it wasn't just Bobby's family that heard his request that night about the green dress. Maybe the enemy was there and heard it too. It's possible that the enemy, for the purpose of laying in Bobby's heart a foundation for doubt and bitterness that would later afflict him, suggested wearing a green dress to an unsuspecting lady choosing her wardrobe that particular morning. It's possible the enemy was using the information he overheard to manipulate circumstances to make it appear God was saying something He wasn't.

A Game Our Enemy Likes to Play

You may be thinking I've chosen an extreme case to illustrate this point. Or you might assume that Satan's limitations would keep him from ever manufacturing any "sign" that we ask for only from God. But from what we see happening with Moses and Aaron as they stood before Pharaoh, this seems to be exactly the kind of game the devil likes to play.

Pharaoh asked Moses and Aaron to perform a miracle; then Aaron, under God's instructions, threw down his rod and it became a serpent. But Pharaoh called in his own sorcerers and magicians, and they did the same thing, most likely by demonic influence. When Aaron later used his rod to turn Egypt's water into blood and to cover the land with frogs, Pharaoh's conjurers again made a show of reproducing both acts (although, with unbloody water hard to find at that point, and frogs already everywhere, perhaps this wasn't so impressive after all).

If "Satan himself transforms himself into an angel of light" (2 Corinthians 11:14), deceptive tricks like that are only to be expected from his forces still today.

RISKY BUSINESS

Consider again those two stories—Gideon's and Bobby's. The fleece worked for one, but not for the other. That should lead us to a clear conclusion: The fleece is risky business at best. It lends itself to second-guessing one's actions after it's too late, and far too many "fleeces" lead only to disappointment and disillusionment.

The important point to keep in mind here is that our clear understanding of God's will in our life is a serious threat to Satan.

To keep us from knowing it, he'll try everything—including imitating providential signs in order to deceive us. It's a sobering truth to realize Satan can mimic God's power and fabricate a set of circumstances for those who would publicly use a fleece to determine God's will. The "signs" they receive after asking God to show them may actually be Satan's counterfeit.

SOMETHING BETTER

For getting a "go" sign from God, there has to be a better approach than the fleece, one that isn't so fraught with inherent uncertainties.

And there is—the secret place. That should be our first destination when we need guidance from our Father. It's there we can pour out our heart and find answers, in the presence of the One who works everything for our good. Shielded there from our enemy, we'll find refreshing strength and wisdom, in the certainty that the plans made with God in the confidentiality of our secret place can't be co-opted by Satan's cronies.

Relying on the secret place instead of attempting shortcuts to finding God's will would help prevent tragic stories like Bobby's.

Some Christians bemoan how "difficult" it is to find God's will. I think I understand the heart of someone who entertains that notion, but in hindsight I've always found His answers to be on time and apparent. They haven't always been to my liking, but they've always been true to His written Word.

Money for a Phone Call

Years ago a young woman in our church approached me after I'd spoken on this subject to tell me about something that had happened in her life. As she began, I first thought she was relating another "fleece" story. But as she continued, I sensed her genuine interest in doing business alone with God through the mystery and intimacy of the secret place.

"I'd been dating this guy my parents didn't approve of," she said. "Since I'm over twenty, I figured I knew what was best. I was blinded by love. But I heard you say in a sermon that the devil couldn't read my thoughts and that I should do business in the secret place, so I took you up on it."

She pondered her parents' objections to this relationship, then decided to take it to the Lord in her secret place. She came up with a plan known only to her and to God.

She was at college, and to break off the relationship would require a long-distance phone call—something she couldn't afford at the time. She felt that asking her parents for the money would violate the spirit of her plan. Instead, she asked God to give her the extra money required. Otherwise she would have to resign herself to waiting for the next time her boyfriend phoned her.

She had a job that barely gave her enough spending money while in school. She worked at a smorgasbord-style cafeteria, where customers rarely gave tips to those doing what she did—

busing tables. But a nice tip, she thought, would probably be enough to pay for the call.

As she related what happened when she next went to work after making her plans with God, she almost shouted: "Can you imagine how my heart jumped? For the first time on my job people left money on the tables! I can't remember that happening again during the eight months I worked there."

She made the phone call that night and ended the relationship. Soon, God brought an outstanding young man into her life. They're now pastoring a church, and she's even authored a couple of books.

From *In the Secret Place,* Chapter 7

CHAPTER 12

WAITING AND LISTENING

RON MEHL

> *Now all Judah, with their little ones, their wives,*
> *and their children, stood before the LORD. Then the Spirit of*
> *the Lord came upon Jahaziel the son of Zechariah,*
> *the son of Benaiah, the son of Jeiel, the son of Mattaniah,*
> *a Levite of the sons of Asaph, in the midst of the assembly. And he*
> *said, "Listen, all you of Judah and you inhabitants of Jerusalem,*
> *and you, King Jehoshaphat! Thus says the Lord to you:*
> *'Do not be afraid nor dismayed because of this great multitude,*
> *for the battle is not yours, but God's.'"*

2 CHRONICLES 20: 13-15

What a picture! *All* Judah stood before the Lord: men and women, husbands and wives, sons and daughters, grandfathers and grandmothers, teenagers and toddlers, and babes in their mothers' arms. Their king had just finished humbling himself and pouring out his heart for his people. His last words had been, "We do not know what to do, but our eyes are upon You."

Then, with nothing left to say, the great assembly fell silent.

And waited.

And listened.

Then the Lord began to speak.

Jehoshaphat could have kept this prayer concern private—just between him and an inner circle of advisors. "After all," he might have reasoned, "we don't want panic in the streets." But he refused to do that. Instead, he assembled the whole nation for a mass prayer meeting. Every man, woman, and child in Judah had a stake in this issue, so their king gathered them all together before the feet of God.

There's something powerful about praying together in a great assembly. Anyone who knows our church in Beaverton will tell you that our Thursday night prayer meeting is the most significant service of the week, and Sunday morning is wonderful, Sunday night is always joyous and encouraging, but Thursday night is where the action is. The building is filled with people kneeling before God and crying out to Him in prayer.

When I recently went through some especially intensive chemotherapy treatments, I ended up having a very bad reaction that put me in the hospital for ten days. It was a serious time, and the pain was greater than anything I've ever experienced in my life. I was given morphine to help alleviate the pain. For ten days, day and night, Joyce sat in a chair next to my bed, helping to administer the morphine every twenty minutes and praying without ceasing. She knew how vulnerable I was in that moment to any potential complications.

I learned later that the whole church family had gathered to pray for me. As with the crisis in Judah, *all* the people gathered. Since those days I've received piles of notes and cards from children who wrote, "Pastor, my mom and dad and I prayed for you every day."

And the Lord did a mighty work. I'm back doing what I love more than anything else in life…back in the pulpit, shepherding the flock I love.

All because God's people prayed.

In the midst of hopeless and impossible times, what is it that moves heaven on our behalf? It's people who pour out their request before Him, then listen for His answer.

I think of the prophet Habakkuk, who cried out to God and spread out his complaint and great burden at the feet of the Lord. Then, when he was done, he didn't budge from his place until he heard the Lord's answer.

> *I will climb up into my watchtower now and wait*
> *to see what the LORD will say to me and how he*
> *will answer my complaint. (Habakkuk 2:1)*

Is that what you do after you've prayed? Do you climb up into your watchtower and wait for the answer? Do you begin to anticipate God's reply and earnestly listen for what He has to say to you and how He will direct you? Or do you hasten off to your activities and plunge back into the world of noise and confusion and ten thousand distractions?

After Habakkuk purposed to wait, the very next verse says, "Then the LORD answered me and said...." (Habakkuk 2:2). Likewise, as Jehoshaphat and Judah waited on the Lord, He answered their prayer. The Bible says, "Then the Spirit of the LORD came upon Jahaziel.... And he said...." (2 Chronicles 20:14–15).

Satan hates it when we pray, and he hates it even more when we wait on the Lord for His direction and help and counsel. Why doesn't he want us to listen to God? Because he wants us to be separated from the Lord. He doesn't want us to connect with Him. He doesn't want us to see God as our Father, as our Provider, or as the All-Powerful One. Our enemy would rather keep us busy—even in the Lord's work, if need be—than see us quiet our souls to listen for God's voice.

It isn't easy taking time to listen. Most of us are wired for action, for doing. Standing and waiting, as Judah did on that historic day, is a challenge for us.

Susanna Wesley, mother to Charles and John Wesley, had seventeen children. Most of us can only imagine how hectic things became in that household. Just think of the incredible noise and confusion two or three kids can generate on a rainy day indoors. How would you like to try on seventeen for size? It would be like running a wild 'n' wooly day-care center single-handedly—only you never get to leave for the quiet of home at night because you *are* home.

One of the most difficult things for this godly woman was finding a time and place to pray each day. Because there were so many children occupying every corner of the house, she had no place to go for a quiet moment, no place to retreat. That's when she came up with this radical solution. She told all the children that when they saw her sitting in the kitchen with her apron pulled up over her head, she was talking to God, and they weren't to disturb her.

That story makes me think of a more contemporary illustration. My friend Amos Dodge told me about his dear mom and her designated prayer place. There were "only" eleven children in the Dodge family, but they didn't have a house. They all lived in a thirty-five-foot travel trailer, which they pulled with one of those huge old Cadillac Fleetwoods.

When life became too hectic and the noise and confusion closed in on her, Mrs. Dodge would slip out to the Cadillac, sit in the backseat, bow her head, and pray. The kids, busy in their games and pursuits, would suddenly miss her and wonder where she'd gone.

Several of them would finally think to look outside, and sure enough, there she would be in the backseat, head bowed, talking to the Lord. Amos told me that the kids knew better than to bother her in that place of retreat. Everyone knew that was Mother's place to be quiet before God. If you didn't want to find yourself in serious trouble, you'd give that old Caddy a wide berth. And the God who sat in the driver's seat of this dear woman's life gave her many remarkable and amazing answers to prayer.

Just one more story. Dr. Eno, one of my professors in Bible college, told us about his morning prayer times when he was a young pastor at a tiny church in Canada. He was just starting in his ministry, and he was trying to adjust to the deep snow and below-zero temperatures.

His flock was small and conditions were harsh, but Dr. Eno was a very godly man who cared deeply about the small flock entrusted into his care. He would always get up at four o'clock in the morning to pray. The little house, of course, was freezing cold in those dark hours before dawn, and their only source of heat was the wood-burning cooking stove in the kitchen.

So Dr. Eno would start a fire in the stove, get down on his knees in that icy kitchen, and put his head into the oven so he could feel the warmth while he prayed. When he told the class that story, I remember how several of us ministry students laughed. It was such a ridiculous picture. A preacher with his head in the oven! Yet as the years have gone by, I don't laugh about that anymore. I know how desperately I need God's strength and wisdom in my life and ministry and how I need to make prayer a priority like Dr. Eno did.

He used to tell us, "You can do a whole lot of things to ready yourself for the ministry. You can read all the books and go to all the classes. But nothing will prepare you for challenging situations like being on your knees every morning of your life."

Now maybe you think it sounds kind of silly to pray with an apron over your face...or in the backseat of an old Cadillac...or with your head in the oven. And maybe it is. But where do *you* pray? How are you making prayer and listening to God a priority in *your* life?

From *A Prayer That Moves Heaven,* Chapter 6

CHAPTER 13

GET ALIGNED
WITH GOD'S WILL

GREG LAURIE

ॐ

Jesus once gave this incredible promise on how to experience answered prayer: "If you abide in Me, and My words abide in you, you will ask what you desire, and it shall be done for you" (John 15:7). This promise could also be translated, "If you maintain a living communion with Me, and My Word is at home with you, I command you to ask at once for whatever your heart desires, and it will be yours."

When I read this passage, I immediately gravitate toward the promise at the end of it. If I ask for whatever my heart desires, it's mine. But then I read more closely what Jesus said before that—a condition to be met: "If you maintain a living communion with Me, and My Word is at home with you."

Wanting What God Wants

To abide like this speaks of intimacy, closeness, and friendship. It's the picture of two friends who are comfortable in each other's presence. You aren't ill at ease with each other, looking forward to getting away. You enjoy being together, and you want to hear what each other has to say.

Now of course this must be balanced with a healthy reverence and awe of who God is. We aren't to become overly casual with Him—He's the Almighty God and He's to be revered, worshiped, and obeyed. But He's also our Father in heaven who greatly desires to hear from us and wants to be our closest and most intimate friend.

Likewise when Jesus says we must let His words abide in us, it means letting the Scriptures be at home in our heart. Therefore our prayers cannot be divorced from our lifestyles. They flow out of a close walk with God. If your life isn't pleasing to God, your effective prayer life will be practically nonexistent.

If that's what is happening in our life—living communion with the Lord and staying at home in His Word—then we're going to want what *He* wants. He'll be changing our outlook, our desires, and eventually our prayers. If we abide in Jesus, we'll grow to the point of being able to "automatically" sense God's will, and so we'll be asking for it in prayer.

His Listening Ear

So the prayer that prevails with God involves something more than sheer gut-it-out persistence. Persevering prayer that's truly effective will always keep bringing us more closely aligned with God's will, as we find ourselves wanting more and more what He wants.

The primary objective of wrestling prayer is to line our will up with the will of God. Only when we do that will we see more of our prayers answered in the affirmative. Nothing lies outside the reach of prayer—except what lies outside the will of God. God answers only the requests which He Himself inspires.

True wrestling prayer is not getting God to move your way; it's getting you to move His way. It's not bending God to my perspective and attitude, but bending myself to His. It doesn't even involve "informing" God of anything, for Jesus told us, "Your Father knows the things you have need of before you ask Him" (Matthew 6:8).

As Martin Luther said, "By our praying we are instructing ourselves more than Him."

Why does God answer our prayers? "We receive from Him anything we ask *because we obey His command and do what pleases Him*" (1 John 3:22).

If you give a listening ear to all of God's commands, He'll give a listening ear to all your prayers to Him. If you'll agree with

Him, He'll agree with you; if you don't yield to Him, He won't yield to you.

Charles Spurgeon said, "When you have great desires for heavenly things, when your desires are such as God approves of, when you want what God wants, then you will have what you like." That's the key—when your desires are such as God approves of. Get your will in alignment with His.

How do you do it? Spend time in God's presence. Live in His Word. Study the Bible; get it into your blood; know it well. Apply what you read there, and let God change your outlook.

A BLANK CHECK FROM GOD

Recall the Canaanite woman with the demon-possessed daughter, and how Jesus eventually said to her, "Let it be to you as you desire" (Matthew 15:28). God doesn't offer a blank check like that to just anyone. If we're thinking only of ourselves or are motivated by greed, we need not apply. But to the humble person who isn't questioning God's will but is rather surrendering to it, God offers such a possibility.

If you had a blank check from God, what would you tell Him you really want?

Is it the salvation of your child, your husband or wife, a friend, or even your enemy? Maybe it has seemed that the more you pray for them, the farther away from God they get. They may be antagonistic, argumentative, hardened against anything you say. You wonder if your prayers are doing any good.

But don't give up. Keep asking, seeking, knocking. You just don't know how much God is already at work. Maybe He's taking them "all the way down" before they'll get the picture and ask for His help up. Maybe their antagonism is actually the result of the Holy Spirit's conviction in their life. We just don't know.

Do you really want to see a spiritual awakening sweep America? Persist in prayer. We can't begin to imagine how much God will do in answer to such pleading.

Remember that there are certain things Satan doesn't want you to pray for. In one sense he doesn't want you to pray for anything. But there are some things he *really* doesn't want you to pray for.

Satan doesn't want us to pray for revival in America because he knows that's the only thing that could turn our people back to God and bring about any lasting moral change. And I doubt Satan wants you to pray for the salvation of any unbelievers you know.

Concerning issues like that, there may be spiritual warfare happening behind the scenes that goes far beyond our capacity to understand. At a time of great spiritual wrestling in Daniel's life, an angel appeared and told the prophet that his prayers had been heard from the first but that the angel had been delayed in coming to Daniel for three weeks because of a struggle with demonic forces that required the help of the archangel Michael (see Daniel 10:12–13). This amazing account is a reminder that God's delays are not necessarily His denials. Those are the times when God is building up our faith.

Never forget that what may appear to be indifference on God's part is nothing of the sort, but rather a barrier that He wishes you to overcome by persistent praying in faith. Those barriers are not meant to drive us away, but to draw us closer.

COME RULE AND REIGN

One day Jesus was praying and when He finished, one of the disciples made a beautiful request: "Lord, teach us to pray" (Luke 11:1).

Jesus answered by giving them the Model Prayer—not merely a prayer to pray, but rather a guide for all prayer, a pattern to follow. Without question it's a powerful prayer, and there's certainly nothing wrong with praying it verbatim.

But it's even more helpful as a pattern to keep in mind as we approach God, especially when engaging in wrestling prayer. When we're feeling called to really "get down to business" with God, that's probably the most important time to remember the nuts and bolts that Jesus says are essential to the process of prayer.

Now, if Jesus had asked *me* to write that Model Prayer instead of teaching it to us Himself, it might start this way:

"Our Father who art in heaven, give us our daily bread." You know, cut to the chase. Let's get down to business. "How are You, Lord? Nice to be with You. *Now here's what I need...*"

That's how we often pray, rushing into God's presence and rattling off our grocery list. So to be honest, maybe we really ought to be saying, "Our Santa who art in heaven..." or "Our vending machine who art in heaven...."

But according to the pattern Jesus gave us, before we utter a single word of personal petition, we should pray for God's kingdom to come and for His will to be done. Only then do we ask Him to give us this day our daily bread.

"Your kingdom come"—that's what Jesus told us to pray. This is a multilevel request with different shades of meaning. It's first of all a request for the return of Jesus to this earth. The word Jesus uses here for "kingdom" doesn't primarily refer to a geographical territory but rather to sovereignty and dominion. When we pray, "Your kingdom come," we're praying for God's rule on earth, which essentially begins when Jesus returns to rule and reign. It's the request reflected in the Bible's closing prayer: "Even so, come, Lord Jesus!" (Revelation 22:20).

And the word translated as "come" indicates a sudden, instantaneous coming. I'm praying "Lord, please come back and do it soon!" Is your life right now in such a spiritual condition that you can pray this? The answer to that question is a real indicator of where you are with God. ·

Is your expectation of the Lord's return alive and well? The Bible says that "everyone who has this hope in Him purifies himself, just as He is pure" (1 John 3:3). The person who is seeking to know God and walking in holiness with Him has every reason to long for His return.

HIS KINGDOM FOR ME

The prayer "Your kingdom come" is also a personal request. With that prayer, I'm asking for the kingdom of God to come in my own life. "For indeed," Jesus said, "the kingdom of God is within you" (Luke 17:21). He was referring to His own presence on that particular day. The kingdom of God speaks of the present rule and reign of Jesus Christ.

With this prayer I'm saying, "Lord, I want Your rule and reign in my life. I want to live by Your principles found in Your Word. I want You to be in charge. I give You the master key to every room in my life."

But know this: We can't pray "Your kingdom come" until we pray "My kingdom go." So when Jesus says, "Seek first the kingdom of God and His righteousness" (Matthew 6:33), He's saying, "In everything you say and do, before anything else, seek first and foremost the rule and reign of God in your life."

So when I pray "Your kingdom come, Your will be done," I'm saying, "Lord, if the personal requests I'm about to ask for are in anyway outside of Your will, overrule them!"

His Kingdom for Others

The prayer "Your kingdom come" is also an evangelistic prayer. It's a request for the salvation of those who don't know the Lord. As His kingdom is ruling and reigning in our own lives, we can have a part in bringing it to others as we pray to that end.

There's no doubt that the will of God includes people coming to believe in Jesus Christ. God is "not willing that any should perish but that all should come to repentance" (2 Peter 3:9).

Jesus Himself modeled this kind of praying for us. Isaiah's messianic prophecy tells us that Christ "made intercession for the transgressors" (Isaiah 53:12). On the Cross Jesus prayed "Father, forgive them, for they do not know what they do" (Luke 23:34).

A striking example of prayer for nonbelievers is shown in the case of Stephen in Acts. As he was being stoned for his bold, uncompromising stand for Jesus, "he knelt down and cried out with a loud voice, 'Lord, do not charge them with this sin.' And when he had said this, he fell asleep" (Acts 7:60).

We know that a young man named Saul of Tarsus was watching all this happen that day. Could it be that Stephen, inspired by the Holy Spirit, might have been praying especially for Saul? So unexpected was the answer to this prayer that when Saul was converted, many of the Christians didn't believe it. Do you know someone right now whom you cannot even imagine becoming a Christian? Start praying for that person! No one is beyond the reach of prayer or the need of salvation.

Paul himself spoke of the prayer burden he had for the Jews to come to Jesus: "My heart's desire and prayer to God for Israel is that they may be saved" (Romans 10:1).

Though it isn't biblical to "claim" someone's salvation—only God knows if and when that person will truly believe—it is *very* biblical for us to pray, and pray a lot, for unbelievers to come to Christ.

His Will Be Done

In the Model Prayer which Jesus gave us, the request "Your kingdom come" is joined with this one: *"Your will be done* on earth as it is in heaven."

This request, too, has a personal aspect to it: "Your will be done in my life, just as it is in heaven."

This request also includes a prayer concern for others, believers and unbelievers alike: "Your will be done in *his* life and in *her* life, just as it is in heaven."

From *Wrestling with God,* Chapter 4

Extol

❧

You shall rejoice in every good thing
which the LORD your God
has given to you and your house.

DEUTERONOMY 26:11

The LORD is my strength and my shield;
my heart trusted in Him, and I am helped;
therefore my heart greatly rejoices,
and with my song I will praise Him.

PSALM 28:7

Continue earnestly in prayer,
being vigilant in it with thanksgiving.

COLOSSIANS 4:2

CHAPTER 14

ABUNDANT ANSWERS

DAVID JEREMIAH

Several years ago when I preached about prayer in Matthew 7, our church's superbly creative drama team came up with a great way to set our minds on what Jesus is saying in that passage.

Here's what we saw and heard that Sunday:

On the stage is a sort of vestibule outlined with filing cabinets. A couple is entering the vestibule, and a man is waiting there for them. From their conversation, we learn that this is the threshold of heaven, and the apostle Peter himself is inviting the couple in.

After a brief discussion, the man asks Peter, "What are all these filing cabinets for?"

Peter explains that inside the filing drawers are inventories of all the unclaimed gifts God was prepared to give His children, yet they failed to request them from Him. "One of these cabinets has a drawer marked for you," Peter says. "And in it are all the things God wanted to give you that you never asked for."

I'll never forget that! If there were a drawer like that in heaven for you and me, how full would it be? Some of us may be shocked in eternity to realize the potential ministry impact we could have had, and the true blessings we could have known, if we'd only just asked God for them.

UNCONDITIONAL PROMISES

After telling us to ask and seek and knock, Jesus goes on in Matthew 7:8 to make some unconditional promises. Notice what He says:

"Everyone who asks..." What's the next word? *Receives.*

"He who seeks..." What's next? *Finds.*

"And to him who knocks, it will be..." Will be what? *Opened.*

Do you see any loopholes in those promises? Does He say there anywhere that God answers some prayers but not others? Does that passage imply that if we pray, God might hear us, or He might not?

No, God's guarantee for us is this: He hears and answers *every* prayer. Ask and receive, seek and find, knock and watch the door open—these are ironclad promises. Now I know that there are other passages in Scripture that teach further guidelines for prayer—things like praying according to God's will, praying in

Jesus' name, and praying in the Spirit. But the fact is, in this passage, Jesus strongly teaches the profound effectiveness of simply asking, without weighing the process down with any restrictions.

In his profound book *With Christ in the School of Prayer,* Andrew Murray says it simply and powerfully: "God means prayer to have an answer." And we see plenty of evidence for that in the pages of God's Word.

Prayer opened the Red Sea.

Prayer brought water from the rock and bread from heaven.

Prayer made the sun stand still.

Prayer brought fire from the sky on Elijah's sacrifice.

Prayer overthrew armies and healed the sick.

Prayer raised the dead.

The same has always been true, down through all the centuries that have followed Bible times. Prayer has paved the way for the conversion of millions of people. Things that we think are impossible, God does when people pray.

Small Prayers Too

And He not only answers big prayers; the little ones get answered too.

I remember a wonderful story about a woman whose young daughter was taken ill one morning at school. After the mother received a call from the school, she picked up her little girl, took her home, and called the doctor and described her daughter's symptoms. The doctor reported that there seemed to be quite an outbreak of this flulike affliction, and because of the number of people coming in to be treated for it, he wouldn't be able to see the girl until later in the afternoon. For the meantime, he suggested an over-the-counter medicine that the mother could pick up to help her daughter.

The mother put her daughter to bed and tucked her in, then told her she was going to the store for the medicine. "I'll be back in just a few minutes," she said.

She rushed to the store and purchased the medicine, but when she returned to the parking lot, she discovered she'd left her keys in the car. Looking through the window, she could see them dangling from the ignition. And the car was locked.

The first response that came to her mind was to use her cell phone and call her daughter to explain that she was going to be delayed. When she did, her daughter told her, "Mommy, get a coat hanger. I've seen on television how they just stick a coat hanger down the window to unlock the door."

The mother went back inside the store and was able to get a wire coat hanger, though she had her doubts about whether it would work. In fact, she felt embarrassed, because she wasn't sure at all how to use the coat hanger to open her car door. But she was a woman of prayer, so as she left the store she lifted up her heart to the heavenly Father: "I don't know what to do, Lord. My keys are locked in the car, and my little girl is home sick. I've got this coat hanger here, but I don't know what to do with it. Please send somebody to help me."

As she finished her prayer, a car immediately pulled up at the curb right where she was standing and dropped off a passenger. The man who got out must be God's answer, the woman concluded, though he didn't seem like the kind of package God would send—he had a rough look and hadn't shaved for some time, and she thought he might be a homeless person. But she said to him, "Sir, can you help me?"

"What's the problem?" he said.

"I locked my keys in the car, and I've got this coat hanger, but I don't know what to do with it."

"Lady," he said, "where's your car?"

She took him to it, and after bending the coat hanger and inserting it over the top of the window, he quickly got the door open.

The mother was so overwhelmed that she put her arms around this scruffy guy and gave him a hug to thank him. "You're such a good man," she told him.

"Lady," he replied, "I'm no good man. I just got out of prison."

As the man walked away, the mother prayed, "Thank You, Lord! You sent me a professional!"

Why God Answers

Why did God answer this woman's prayer in such a pointed way for her? Why does he answer any of our prayers?

Oswald Chambers, in his typically pointed style, wrote this in his book *If You Will Ask:*

> *There is only one kind of person who can really pray, and that is the child-like saint, the simple, stupid, supernatural child of God; I do mean "stupid."*

Well, I don't know about you, but I guess that means I qualify as someone who can pray! Chambers then goes on to say that it's "nonsense" to try and use mental reasoning to explain why God answers those "stupid" prayers. "God answers prayer," he writes, "on the ground of redemption and on no other ground. Let us never forget that our prayers are heard, not because we are in earnest, not because we suffer, but because Jesus suffered."

His point about redemption gets a lot of support from the book of Hebrews, where we're reminded that it's "by the blood of Jesus" that we have "boldness" to enter God's presence with our prayers (Hebrews 10:19). The mystery of why God answers prayer is all wrapped up in the mystery of why He redeemed us; just like the Cross, it points to an infinite love that is far beyond any human explanation.

Remembering What God Does

Since I started keeping a journal years ago and writing down my requests, it has been thrilling for me to look back to see what God has done in my life in response to my prayers. Again and again I see how God will eventually answer requests that I had almost forgotten about. Sometimes the answers are so specific that it's almost frightening. To think that God, the Ruler of the universe, would do that for me for no other reason than that I asked! It staggers me.

Seeing repeated answers has got to be one of the most powerful motivators to continued prayer. If you're like me, it's easy to overlook or forget what God has done for you.

One year as I approached yet another birthday, I was feeling very low. Then one day I received a birthday card from a friend and a member of our church. He did more than wish me a happy birthday; he included a note that recounted for me some of the blessings I'd experienced since my last birthday:

> *Healed from a terrible disease, sold a house and built a new one (no mean feat in these challenging times), had a son do remarkably well on the football field and win a county championship, had a daughter get married, had a radio program grow to major proportions, got a son and daughter-in-law*

back to California and into a new home, preached
wonderful sermons each Sunday several times to a
huge number of people, led a vibrant school system
(preschool through college), managed a complex
system of ministries (from in-home Bible studies to
missionaries throughout the world)...and the list
goes on and on. And this from the perspective of
one who just sees a small part of what is happening
from a seat in the congregation.

Reading that pulled me out of the doldrums. I knew that all of those things on that long list had been items for prayer in the previous year. I could only thank the Lord for allowing me another year of life on earth and for being so gracious and helpful to me in all that He had accomplished in my life.

ASKING AND GETTING

R. A. Torrey has written some of the best books on prayer every published, but there was a time when his prayer life couldn't get off the ground. Then a day came, Torrey writes, "when I realized what real prayer meant, realized that prayer was having an audience with God, actually coming into the presence of God, and asking and getting things from Him."

That realization transformed his prayer life.

Before that, prayer had been a mere duty, and sometimes a very irksome duty, but from that time on prayer has been not merely a duty, but a privilege, one of the most highly esteemed privileges of life.

Before that the thought that I had was, "How much time must I spend in prayer?" The thought that now possesses me is, "How much time may I spend in prayer without neglecting the other privileges and duties of life?"

As you get a deeper and deeper picture of how prayer means being in the presence of God to both ask for and receive His blessings, I hope that you too will begin to find it one of the highest privileges in your life.

_____

From *The Prayer Matrix*, Chapter 2

CHAPTER 15

GIVING GLORY TO GOD

SHIRLEY DOBSON

A few years ago, Jim and I attended a University of Southern California football game. On a beautiful Saturday afternoon we entered venerable Los Angeles Memorial Coliseum and settled into our seats, enjoying the anticipation of a festive afternoon. Thousands of fans joined us, many displaying the latest in USC apparel. The marching band performed several popular tunes. Then a regal Trojan warrior appeared astride a white horse. The warrior thrust his sword skyward; together, man and horse charged across the field to the roar of the crowd.

The stage was set. At one end of the field, a huge mass of players in cardinal and gold uniforms and helmets huddled together. The crowd buzzed expectantly. Suddenly, the players raced en masse toward the center of the field as the band burst into the USC fight song. The crowd (two Dobsons included) rose as one and delivered a thunderous ovation for the young heroes. Fans clapped, raised their arms, and voiced their admiration at the top of their lungs. The power and enthusiasm of that greeting must have been heard for miles!

I don't remember many details about the game itself. But I do recall the conversation that Jim and I had afterward about our collective display of adoration. For thousands of us, the exhilaration we felt when the USC team ran onto the field was total and genuine. But a question nagged at me: If we can respond like this to a group of college student-athletes, how much more awe and enthusiasm should we be willing to show to our heavenly Father?

It's important to remember that God is not our "genie in a bottle"—He is not simply waiting in heaven to receive our laundry list of self-centered requests. On the contrary, God is worthy of our praise and is pleased when we come before Him with thanksgiving. He wants to be appreciated, just as we do.

Praise and adoration are not merely "appetizers" in the lives of believers—they are part of the main course. David, who gave us so many wonderful words of praise in the Psalms, put it this way: "Ascribe to the LORD the glory due his name.... Worship the LORD in the splendor of his holiness" (1 Chronicles 16:29).

In the same way, praise and worship are essential to an effective and satisfying life of prayer. When Jesus taught His disciples how they should pray, He *began* with praise: "Our Father in heaven, *hallowed be your name*" (Matthew 6:9).

We would be wise to keep this in mind when we pray. After all, our God is the sovereign Creator of the universe! He loves us as His own children and has provided every good thing we have; He is worthy of our praise every moment. Yet I know that many of you are facing frustrations and trials and sorrows that threaten to overwhelm you. Your hope and faith are still in the Lord, but right now you just don't *feel* very worshipful. You may be thinking: *Shouldn't I wait until the feeling returns to offer Him my praise? Isn't that more genuine?*

Here is my suggestion: Instead of waiting for the feeling, wait upon God. You can do this by growing still and quiet, then expressing in prayer what your mind knows is true about Him, even if your heart doesn't feel it at this moment. Be honest. Tell the Lord how much you need His presence in your cold, empty heart to rekindle and ignite your praise for Him. In faith, invite the Lord to fill your heart—then wait until He does.

When we make this sincere effort to give our hearts and minds to God, we draw near to Him—and He draws near to us, just as He promised (see Hebrews 10:22–23). We begin to taste His refreshing water that soothes our inner thirst. We start to see how perfectly capable He is of handling our cares and concerns, which suddenly seem much smaller. We finally relax and focus fully on praising Him.

Inspiration for Adoration

There are other ways to rediscover adoration for the Lord. The most obvious source is the pages of Scripture. The Psalms, especially, are filled with marvelous descriptions and examples of praise to our heavenly Father. Psalm 89 begins, "I will sing of the LORD's great love forever; with my mouth I will make your faithfulness known through all generations."

We can also turn to songs of praise in a hymnbook, as well as to many excellent books that explore God's character and attributes. Of course, worshiping with fellow believers at church can be a tremendous source of inspiration. Setting aside regular family times for praise and worship may also bring out heartfelt moments of heavenly acclamation.

In the Dobson household, one of our favorite traditions at both Thanksgiving and Christmas has been for family members to share at least one blessing from the past year for which they are especially thankful. It is a time for appreciating each other and God; typically, many of us are in tears before we're done! These moments always remind us just how much God has given us all.

Author Ruth Myers writes, "I find that my worship is richer when I offer the Lord praise and thanks for three things: *who He is, what He does, and what He gives.*"

At this very moment, what can you say about each of these? I urge you to review often the questions of who God is, what He does, and what He gives. I pray that your answers every day will be a little richer, a little stronger, and a little more powerful in the grip they hold on your heart's affections.

The Pleasure Is His

God is most worthy of our praise—yet we have another reason to worship Him. He invites us into conversation with Him because it brings Him *pleasure*.

That's sometimes a little hard to believe, isn't it? The holy and perfect and all-powerful ruler of the universe *enjoys* our prayers of praise? But the proof is in Scripture: "The prayer of the upright is His delight" (Proverbs 15:8). God actually delights in and *pursues* our worship. As Jesus said, "A time is coming and has now come when the true worshipers will worship the Father in spirit and truth, for they are *the kind of worshipers the Father seeks*" (John 4:23).

It always thrills my heart to read those verses! It is overwhelming to think that when I worship Him in spirit and truth, God is actively seeking *me*. That brings an excitement to my worship, whether in church or in private prayer.

When you build on the enthusiasm that grows from this kind of worship, your entire life can become a song of praise to God. In His perfect plan, your existence in this life, and for all eternity, will bring Him glory just as He promised. You can even say, as David did, "I will praise you, O Lord my God, with all my heart; I will glorify your name forever" (Psalm 86:12).

Scripture promises that the whole of creation will be filled with His glory. In this very moment, today, your praise to Him can be part of that glory. By speaking to Him, by singing, even by worshiping Him in adoring silence, you and I can offer our very own praise to Almighty God. What an honor and privilege!

THE PLEASURE IS ALSO OURS

The pleasure of our praise and prayers will always be God's— but there is indescribable pleasure in these acts for us as well. Our worship is more than a duty. It's a deed that generates a deeply satisfying joy.

It's actually quite striking to see how closely joy is linked with prayer in New Testament teaching:

> *Be joyful in hope, patient in affliction, faithful in prayer. (Romans 12:12)*
> *Be joyful always; pray continually; give thanks in all circumstances, for this is God's will for you in Christ Jesus. (1 Thessalonians 5:16–18)*
> *Rejoice in the Lord always. I will say it again: Rejoice! Let your gentleness be evident to all. The Lord is near. Do not be anxious about anything,*

*but in everything, by prayer and petition, with
thanksgiving, present your requests to God. And the
peace of God, which transcends all understanding,
will guard your hearts and your minds in Christ
Jesus. (Philippians 4:4–7)
In all my prayers for all of you, I always pray with joy.
(Philippians 1:4)*

No part of our prayers creates a greater feeling of joy than
when we praise God for who He is. He is our Master Creator,
our Father, our source of all love. Every breath we take is a gift
from His hand. When we focus on Him, we move from being
self-centered, with worry and distress, to being God-centered,
with joy and peace in our hearts.

––––––––––––

From *Certain Peace in Uncertain Times,* Chapter 2

Ways to Grow in Prayer

Ruth Myers

❧

Prayer can help bring rich and satisfying renewal to our lives. But it's not simply a nice addition we decide to track onto a luke-warm and stunted spiritual life. Prayer won't grow well by itself.

To benefit fully through prayer, we must plant it in a well-watered garden, where it will grow along with other spiritual atti-tudes and practices. If any of these are missing, weeds grow up and choke our prayer life, making it more of a burden than a blessing.

In the following pages, we consider eight vital areas of our spiritual life that significantly affect praying. Only as we nurture a growing relationship with the Lord can our prayer life thrive.

1. Cultivate Faith Through Pursuing God

Faith is trusting God—counting on Him to be who He says He is and to do what He says He will do. Picture a man who is a tremendous husband—an excellent provider, strong and affectionate, a good listener, eager to help, excellent with the children, honest, and faithful to his wife. Would we be surprised if his wife trusted him? Of course not. Rather, we'd be amazed if she didn't.

We're often amazed when we meet someone who has a deep faith in God. But God is stronger, more loving, more eager to help, more faithful, and infinitely more wonderful than the best husband in the world. Why don't we trust Him more? Because we don't know Him well. Perhaps we haven't put Him to the test through obedience and prayer, and then watched Him keep His word. We're left to suffer from not knowing Him and from the resulting misconceptions that strangle our faith.

But we can change this. We can study the Scriptures day by day with the earnest prayer, "Lord, show me what You are like. By Your Spirit impress truths about You on my heart. Use Your Word to clear out my wrong ideas and to plant deep in my heart a true knowledge of You."

For years my husband and I have made a rewarding pastime of collecting Bible verses about God. What treasures we have come across thus far! And we've only just begun. We search out and savor passages that tell us about God's holiness. His supreme majesty and perfect purity. His righteousness. His truthfulness.

We've learned more about how wise He is, how loving, how powerful, how worthy of our trust.

Our goal is to understand God better and value Him more. We meditate on the passages, seeking to let the Holy Spirit grip our hearts with them. Why not join us? Record your discoveries. Perhaps start a notebook where you can write down exciting truths about God for years to come.

Your faith will flourish as you focus on God and praise Him for how awesome and wonderful He is. You might want to begin with the following passages. Exodus 15:6–7, 11; Deuteronomy 32:4; I Chronicles 29:11–13; Jeremiah 10:6–7, 12; 31:3; 32:17, 27; Lamentations 3:22–23; Daniel 4:35; Zephaniah 3:17; Revelation 15:3–4.

Ask the Lord for a growing thirst for Him. Pray often about this, for yourself and for others. Begin with A. W. Tozer's prayer from *The Pursuit of God*.

> *O God, I have tasted Your goodness, and it has*
> *both satisfied me and made me thirsty for more…*
> *O God, the Triune God, I want to want You;*
> *I long to be filled with longing… Show me Your*
> *glory, I pray, so that I may know You indeed…*
> *Give me grace to rise and follow You up from this*
> *misty lowland where I have wandered so long.*
> *In Jesus' name, Amen.*

2. Count on the Truth of Instant Forgiveness

When we sense we are living in obedience to God, it's easier to pray with confidence. But what about the times when we haven't been trusting and obeying the Lord? Or the times when we think, *I've confessed my sin, yet my conscience still bothers me— and my confidence is still shattered?* In times like that, we tend to avoid prayer, or we come before God like a puppy with its tail between its legs.

How can we regain our confidence?

First of all, be assured that the Lord is always eager to forgive and cleanse you. He longs for you to confess your sins, including your lack of trust, and to reaffirm your commitment to Christ as your Lord. Think of confession as part of maintaining a healthy relationship with God and an essential part of your obedience. Another part of your obedience is to count on the fact that the Lord has kept His promise to forgive you and immediately relates to you just as if you had never sinned!

A powerful Scripture that can help you grow in this area is 1 John 1:9: "If we confess our sins, he is faithful and just and will forgive us our sins and purify us from all unrighteousness." Other passages are Psalm 32:5; Proverbs 28:13; Psalm 130:3–4; and Romans 4:7–8.

Immediately after you confess, you can pray with boldness before God! When you forget this and get trapped in self-condemnation, be encouraged by the response of the devout Frances of Sales, sixteenth-century Bishop of Geneva: "Well my poor soul, here we are in the ditch again, in spite of our earnest resolve to stay out of it. Ah well, let us get out and go on our way, and we'll do well enough, God helping us."

Don't let vague guilt hinder your prayers. Satan likes to attack us with a general, condemning accusing sense of sinfulness and failure—that's why he is described as "the accuser of our brothers" (Revelation 12:10). In contrast, when the Holy Spirit convicts us of sin He is specific. He is firm and persistent but also gentle. He's not out to condemn us but to liberate us and draw us back into fellowship with God.

If you find yourself oppressed by a thick cloud of vague guilt, remember that God is not in the business of condemning His children. That's the devil's business. So choose to resist him. Thank the Father that Satan is a defeated enemy, that Jesus is Victor over him, and that you need not be taken in by his oppression and lies. Thank the Father that His Son bore all your guilt on the cross and that now your true self is clean and righteous. Praise Him that He does not treat you as your sins deserve, for His love and mercy are as high as the heavens are above the earth. Then go on with your interceding, asking the

Holy Spirit to show you clearly if there's any specific sin He wants you to confess.

After we confess our sin, we should resist any urge to scold or punish ourselves. This is our self-centered, worldly way of trying to buy forgiveness or reform ourselves. The pathway back to obedience is seeing ourselves as forgiven and cleansed and able to conquer sin by Christ's holy and powerful life within us.

Other passages that may help you are Romans 8:1; 2 Corinthians 2:13–15; and Psalm 103:10–13.

3. ABIDE IN CHRIST

Hudson Taylor, a great missionary to China during the 1800s, had been groping through a period of dense darkness. He felt overwhelmed by his failures and inadequacy and lack of power. He knew that all he needed was in Christ—but the big question he wrestled with was how to get it out of Christ and into himself.

Then, through a letter from a coworker, the Lord opened Taylor's eyes to see that he was so united to Christ that he shared His life. He was simply to accept Christ's invitation to "abide in Me" and not try to get anything out of Him. He wrote to his sister:

> *How great seemed my mistake in wishing to get the sap, the fullness out of Him!... The vine is not*

the root merely, but all—root, stem, branches,
twigs... And Jesus is not that alone—He is oil and
sunshine, air and showers, and ten thousand times
more than we have ever dreamed, wished for, or
needed. Oh, the joy of seeing this truth! Can Christ
be rich and I poor? Can your head be well fed
while your body starves?

"Abide in Me"—what an incredible invitation! Jesus (think of who He is!) wants an intimate relationship with us, a relationship of mutual enjoyment, with us living in Him and He is us. Abiding in Christ means to depend on Him, enjoying our spiritual union with Him and allowing Him to meet our needs.

"Abiding" is a basic preparation for praying the way God want us to pray. Think of the ;promise in John 15:7, "If you abide in Me, and My words abide in you, ask whatever you wish, and it shall be done for you." As your hand experiences the life of your body as its own, so as you abide in Christ you experience the life of Christ as your own. Life that is fresh, pure, joyous, fruitful, free of anxiety, and full of faith. Life that is wrapped up in the desires that are on God's heart. Then when you pray, you express His longings; you want what He wants. And so He does what you ask.

Abiding is not complicated or strenuous. It's as simple as the new birth. The Holy Spirit did His quiet work within us, making us ready to trust Christ. Then we acknowledged our need. We turned from depending on our won works and worthiness, and yielded to Christ as the one source of forgiveness and eternal life. We trusted in Him as our Lord and Savior with no conscious reservations. The scenario and feelings were different for each of us. But two things were the same: the turning and the trusting.

Abiding in Christ is much the same, except that it requires God's continual working, not His once-for-all work. We are "in Christ"—we don't have t try to get there; and the words "in Christ" could be translated "in union with Christ." We simply agree to a constant dependence on Him. We turn, time and again, from our own abilities, our own sufficiency, and our own pride that wants to do it on our own. We accept His word, "Without Me you can do nothing"—that is, nothing significant in God's eyes.

We turn, and we trust.

We choose to depend on Christ as our constant source of life, our constant source of all we need for living and growing, for bearing spiritual fruit, for praying. Then we trust Him to keep us trusting and ask Him to help us turn back quickly whenever we slip into going our own way, doing our own thing, or depending on our own resources. We can keep our trust more constant by saying often, "Thank You that You are my life!"

The Bible reveals that the Triune God is committed to our abiding in Christ! The Holy Spirit prepares us day by day so that

Christ can dwell in our hearts by faith (Ephesians 3:16–17). Our Father, as the Vinekeeper, watches over us every moment, day and night, watering us, protecting us, and pruning us so that we bear much fruit (John 15:1–3; Isaiah 27:3).

Our part is simply to say yes to our Lord's invitation to abide in Him. Pray:

> *Lord, what a privilege! What an honor!*
> *And I say yes! I want to abide in You now and all*
> *my life. I choose to turn to You as my master*
> *and as my life, my all-sufficient source. I choose to*
> *trust You to live Your life in me. I choose to rest*
> *in You and live in loving fellowship with You.*
> *And I count on You to make my abiding more and*
> *more constant. Keep me trusting in You, and draw*
> *me back quickly whenever I slip into trusting my*
> *own strength and going my own way.*

Here's a simple prayer from an old poem that we find helpful:

> *Live out Your life within me, O Jesus, King of kings.*
> *Be You Yourself the answer to all my questionings.*

We like to add:

And be the answer, Lord, to all my needs, including
my need to pray as You desire.

We enjoy Andrew Murray's description of abiding: "Abiding in Jesus is nothing but the giving up of oneself to be ruled and taught and led, and so resting in the arms of Everlasting Love."

Years after Hudson Taylor learned the secret of abiding in Christ, someone asked him if he was always conscious of abiding in Christ. He replied, "While sleeping last night, did I cease to abide in your home because I was unconscious of the fact? We should never be conscious of not abiding in Christ."

What a difference it makes in our praying when we abide in Christ!

4. WALK HUMBLY WITH YOUR GOD

If we want God to work in us and for us, answering our prayers, then humility is not merely a nice extra. It's indispensable. "God opposes the proud but gives grace to the humble... Blessed are the destitute and helpless in the realm of the spirit, for theirs is the kingdom of heaven" (James 4:6; Matthew 5:3). No wonder one of the major things God requires of us is to walk humbly with our God (Micah 6:8). If we don't, God will oppose us. We cannot pray as the Lord desires if we're not aware of our true neediness.

Humility has nothing to do with being weak or pessimistic. It's simply thinking about God and ourselves realistically. As we choose humility, God gives us special grace to pray in ways that please Him.

How often we slip into self-sufficiency, leaning on our natural wisdom and abilities, our own power and forcefulness, our own whatever. That's pride. But it can just as easily be pride when we bemoan our weaknesses or lack of natural abilities. You see, either way we're caught in human values that measure us by our abilities and personality rather than by God's evaluation.

What is true humility? Think of it as a two-sided coin. On the one side, genuine humility accepts Jesus' pronouncement, "Without Me you can do nothing" (John 15:5). On the other side of the same reality, genuine humility declares with glad confidence, "I have strength for all things in Christ Who empowers me [I am ready for anything and equal to anything through Him Who infuses inner strength into me]" (John 15:5; Philippians 4:13).

Humility says, like the cherished hymn, "I need You. Oh, I need You!" Then it lets faith take over with the glad affirmation: "I have You! Oh, I have You!" Far more than we know, we are needy persons. Yet we're fully supplied persons as we humbly trust in Him.

In ourselves, by our own abilities and wisdom, we are completely unable to do anything that pleases God. Knowing this prepares us to yield to Christ and trust Him as our life and our sufficiency. Most of us require frequent reminders of our needs and failures; these prod us into humbling ourselves enough to trust God. Sometimes we need the rug pulled out from under us. WE have to fall on our faces so that the truth of our total need for God becomes more than just words. This point of personal poverty is a place of profit; there the wonder of abiding in Christ and the relief of living by His life can begin to dawn in our hearts. Only then can we begin to live and love and pray as He desires. Only then can we take hold of His strength and experience His grace in abundance.

Our failures and unmet needs are in reality great blessings in disguise. They remind us that we're not qualified to run our own lives. They press us to commit ourselves to Christ and trust in Him. They keep us humble. And humility is the only realistic way that we, mere humans, can relate to our supreme and holy God. So make it a practice to bow often before the Lord with a repentant, humble spirit (Isaiah 57:15).

Why does God hate pride? Because it's an empty lie. It's a false confidence that blocks His children's connection with the only solution to their deepest needs. And pride brings immense loss to God because it deprives Him of the genuine intimacy with us that He longs for.

There's no other way to talk with God but to walk humbly. And, as we humble ourselves and honor God, we qualify for the promise, "Those who honor Me I will honor" (1 Samuel 2:30). He will honor us, and He will also honor our prayers.

5. DEPEND ON THE WORD, NOT FEELINGS

Do you feel at times that your prayers just seem to bounce off the ceiling? Nearly everyone does. Even people who are walking with God with no unconfessed sin in their lives experience this. Sometimes they feel their prayers are really "getting through"; at other times they feel their words are going nowhere. Are such feelings an indicator of how God views our prayers?

We get in trouble when we depend on our feelings in prayer. WE start thinking we have to be in a praying mood to pray, or we call our petitions "good prayers" if they give us a certain feeling. It's much better to just decide to pray as God commands—regardless of how we feel. Charles Spurgeon wrote, "We should pray when we are in a praying mood, for it would be sinful to neglect so fair an opportunity. We should pray when we are not in a praying mood because it would be dangerous to remain in so unhealthy a condition."

It's not that feelings are out of place. Many people, in Bible times and since, have prayed with a deep sense of distress or urgency. The afflicted man in Psalm 102 prayed with loud groaning, "My heart is blighted and withered like grass… I am like a desert owl, like an owl among the ruins." If we have deep troubles, God tells us to pour out our hearts to Him (Psalm 62:8). If he gives us intense concern for others, we're to pray with intense feelings. If He makes us particularly conscious of His presence, let's enjoy it. And if the Spirit carries us along in prayer, let's be grateful. But if not, we can still pray, depending on the Word, like the jet pilot who depends on what the instruments say rather than how he feels. We can't judge the success of our prayers by our emotions. And we're not to let our emotions determine whether or not we pray.

Leaving our feelings in God's hands helps us be more consistent in prayer. If we find ourselves floundering, we can ask the Lord to give us insight as we conduct a "heart checkup":

Am I yielding to Christ's lordship and abiding in Him?

Have I confessed every known sin?

Am I praying in Jesus' name—in His merits and not my own?

Am I praying in agreement with what I understand to be God's will and purposes?

Am I praying in faith based on God's Word?

If these checkup questions show that our hearts are right, we can depend on God's promises to hear and answer us. He says in Jeremiah 33:3, "Call to Me, and I will answer you." We can pray "in the Spirit," directed and helped by Him, and depending on the Word He inspired—no matter how we feel.

Christians vary greatly in how they generally feel when they pray. Some have intense emotions; others are more subdued. Resist the urge to compare your feelings in prayer with how others pray. God has made you unique. How you pray—and how you feel as you pray—will also be unique to you and special to God.

Remember that fluctuating emotions are a normal part of being human. Our physical lives move in cycles that affect our emotions, with peaks of high energy and troughs low energy. So when God seems to have disappeared as far as your feelings go, you honor Him in a unique way when you pray anyway.

If you are troubled about an overall lack of positive emotions during prayer, bring your concern to God. Ask Him to overcome any patterns of living or thinking that may be hindering you. But don't get trapped in the error of our feelings-centered age. Feelings are not the only authentic part of our inner person. And being honest in the scriptural sense does not mean expressing all our feelings or responding to all our emotional impulses and preferences. We also have a mind and a will. We can turn our minds to God's commands and with our will choose to obey, even when our feelings don't cooperate. We please God when we choose to let Him and His Word, rather than feelings, govern us.

Hudson Taylor received amazing answers to prayer. Someone asked him late in life if he always felt joyful when he prayed. He replied that his heart usually felt like wood when he prayed and that most of his major victories came through "emotionless prayer."

Yet our emotions matter greatly to God, and He doesn't ask us to ignore them. When your emotions are unpleasant or absent, don't equate this with sin. Jesus Himself expressed troubled emotions in His prayer life. So tell God how you feel and give your emotions to Him. Then choose to bring Him joy by letting Him, not your feelings, govern your prayer choices.

6. LEARN TO BE STILL BEFORE GOD

How can we prepare our hearts for prayer? By cultivating a quiet heart before the Lord, both in our times alone with Him and throughout our days. By letting Him lead us beside still waters.

Moses wrote in Deuteronomy 4:39, "Acknowledge and take to heart this day that the LORD is God in heaven above and on the earth below." We're to think about the truths God has revealed about Himself, poring over them attentively. Then we're to pause and be still—relax, let go, cease striving—and know in the depths of our being that this awesome, exalted, dependable person is God (Psalm 46:10). We can let our thoughts about His greatness lead us to an inner stillness that absorbs His reality and responds to Him with relaxed confidence.

"In returning and rest you shall be saved; in quietness and confidence shall be your strength" we read in Isaiah 30:15. Then at the end of chapter 40, Isaiah tells us that those who wait expectantly on the Lord will renew their strength. Waiting on God and resting in Him have much in common. Both result in absorbing His strength; both involve truly tuning in to God and His Word. The more we have His Word dwelling richly in our hearts, the more it can help us be quiet, restful, and attentive to Him during all our waking hours.

Prayer is conversation, not just monologue. We're to listen as well as speak God's voice is often "still" and "small" and we can easily drown it out. By waiting in quietness before Him, we express our respect and adoration, and we let Him speak to our hearts. He may speak through a sense of His nearness, His love, His welcome, His power, His guidance. He may bring to mind Scriptures that speak to our need.

The strength we absorb from the Lord and the quietness of heart He gives prepare us to pray effectively. We're able to come before God with an alive expectancy rather than wearily dragging ourselves into His presence—though dragging ourselves wearily into His presence is a good thing to do when necessary! But it will be necessary less often as we let God drain away our inner stress and infuse us with His strength day by day.

7. Pray with a Nonjudgmental Attitude

When we intercede without love, we pray without power—we are "only a resounding gong or a clanging cymbal" (1 Corinthians 13:1, NIV). And a common form of lovelessness is a judgmental spirit. How easily, even when we pray with deep concern for others, we can allow a critical attitude to creep in.

John Hyde, a missionary to India so noted for his prayer life that he was called Praying Hyde became burdened to pray for an Indian pastor. Thinking of the pastor's coldness and the resulting deadness of his church, Hyde began to pray: "O Father, You know how cold…" Before he could finish the sentence, the words came to mind, "He who touches him, touches the apple of My eye" (see Zechariah 2:8). Hyde cried out for God to forgive him for being, like Satan, an accuser of a believer—even in prayer.

Hyde decided to turn his thoughts from the negatives that were temporarily true in his fellow servant to the things that were both true and admirable. He asked God to show him all that deserved praise in the pastor's life. Much came to mind, and Hyde spent his prayer time thanking and praising God for his Indian brother. Shortly afterward he learned that, at the very time he was praising and giving thanks, his brother in Christ experienced spiritual renewal. The pastor's life and preaching took on new power.

Sin is fleeting in the lives of God's children. It won't last forever. It is not part of our new nature. In Christ we are cleansed and complete, and God has committed Himself to finish the good work He has begun in us. We can pray for each other's spiritual needs, asking God to deliver. But especially when we're asking God to deliver. But especially when we're asking God to overcome negative qualities, we must be on guard against the sin of a critical, proud spirit cloaked in prayer.

Have you noticed that Paul's recorded prayers for believers—even those who needed correction—were filled not with negative requests but with thanksgiving and positive requests, with the things he wanted to see in their lives? In Philippians 1:9 he did not say, "I pray you'll get over your quarrelling," but "I pray that your love for each other will overflow more and more." (See also Ephesians 3:16–19; Philippians 1:9–11; Colossians 1:9–12; and 1 Corinthians 1:4–8.) When we're concerned about a person's negative qualities, it helps to think through to the corresponding positive qualities we hope for, and pray for those. We personally find it easier to have faith for the positives than against the negatives.

8. View Prayer As a Way of Life

The habit of quietly turning in to God helps us obey His command, "Pray continually," or "Keep on praying" (1 Thessalonians 5:17).

How can we pray all the time when so many things demand our attention? What does this command really mean?

Could it mean that apart from our times set apart for prayer, much of our praying is a simple awareness of the Lord, with an attitude of dependence or gratitude, with a quiet, almost wordless sense of communion? This God-centered attitude is an outgrowth of our abiding in Christ. It prepares us to bring requests to the Lord as they come to mind throughout the day, for both tiny and giant things. In other words, we include our best, our heavenly Friend, in our daily experiences rather than just ignoring Him. Sometimes we sort of mumble casual remarks or a simple "Yes Lord" that acknowledges His presence. At other times we voice a "Thank You" or a quiet "Hallelujah." Sometimes we share with Him an ongoing conversation about our thoughts and feelings, our concerns and desires.

As we abide in Christ, our minds are like the hand of a scale that points upward unless something is being weighed. In a similar way, our thoughts can be aware of the Lord, with an upward focus, except when something needs our full attention—some task, some social interaction. Even then we can now and then direct quick "arrow" prayers to the Lord about what we are doing—sometimes just a glance of our mind His way that says, "I need help."

When the need for immediate focus on the task at hand passes, turning our fuller attention to the Lord is again possible. We can once more lift to Him our love, as well as our needs, reminding Him that we're depending on Him. This means we'll be available to intercede whenever the Lord brings mind some person or need or situation, near or far.

Don't most of us need to pray more constantly? This suggests an important "change me" request. Pray (now and often) that the Lord will help you turn your heart to Him more frequently throughout the day and that this will develop into praying continually. Ask Him to overcome anything in you that hinders a constant, quiet, prayerful spirit—anything that divides your heart or diverts you from communion with your Lord.

Also pray that you will turn to God more often with short arrow prayers—prayers that rise to God throughout your waking hours for people you see, people you relate to, and people who come to mind. Does someone remind you of a friend? Does the news tell of people in need? Use these daily promptings to release quick, on-the-spot prayers.

> *I cannot tell why there should come to me*
> *A thought of someone miles and years away.*
> *In swift insistence on the memory,*
> *Unless there is a need that I should pray.*

Perhaps just then my friend has fiercer fight,
A more appalling weakness, a decay
Of courage, darkness, some lost sense of right;
And so, in case he needs my prayers I pray.

ROSALIND GOFORTH

While on earth Jesus prayed continually. Before feeding the five thousand, at the raising of Lazarus, before choosing His disciples, with His disciples, for His disciples, all night, early in the morning, in the garden, on the cross—Jesus prayed. Prayer was a way of life to Him and still is today as He continually intercedes for us.

Prayer will become a more constant, more treasured part of our lives, too, as we become more like the Lord.

———————

From *31 Days of Prayer,* Part 3